ITALIAN

in 10 minutes a day®

by **Kristine Kershul**, M.A., University of California, Santa Barbara

adapted by Karen Manarolla Nordquist

Published by
Bilingual Books, Inc.
6018 Seaview Avenue N.W.
Seattle, Washington 98107
Telephone: (206) 789-7544
Telex: 499 6629 BBKS UI

Distributed by
USA: Cliffs Notes, Box 80728, Lincoln, Nebraska 68501
UK: Ruskin Book Services, 15 Comberton Hill, Kidderminster,
      Worcestershire DY10 1QG
Copyright © 1981, 1988 by Kristine Kershul and Bilingual Books, Inc.
All rights reserved. (ISBN 0-944502-31-8) 8-7-1-2

L'alfabeto
(lahl-fah-beh-toh)

Many Italian letters sound the same as they do in English, but some Italian letters are pronounced or written differently. To learn the Italian sounds of these letters, write each example in the space provided, in addition to saying each word many times. After you practice the word, see if you can locate it on the map.

Italian letter	English sound	Example	(Write it here)
a	ah	Catania *(kah-tah-nee-ah)*	
c *(before a,o,u and all consonants)*	k	Como *(koh-moh)*	
ch	k	Marche *(mahr-keh)*	*Marche*
c *(before e,i)*	ch	Sicilia *(see-chee-lee-ah)*	
ci *(before a,o,u)*	ch	Francia *(frahn-chah)*	
e	eh *(as in let)*	Tevere *(teh-veh-reh)*	
g *(before a,o,u)*	g *(as in go)*	Garda *(gahr-dah)*	
gh	g *(as in spaghetti)*	Alleghe *(ahl-leh-geh)*	
g *(before e,i)*	j *(as in John)*	Genova *(jeh-noh-vah)*	
gi *(before a,o,u)*	j *(as in John)*	Reggio *(reh-joh)*	
gli	l-y *(as in million)*	Puglia *(pool-yah)*	
gn	n-y *(as in onion)*	Bologna *(boh-lohn-yah)*	
i	ee	Pisa *(pee-sah)*	
o	oh	Po *(poh)*	
r	*(slightly rolled)*	Roma *(roh-mah)*	
s *(beginning a word and followed by a consonant)*	z	Svizzera *(zvee-tseh-rah)*	
sc *(before a,o,u)*	sk	Toscana *(toh-skah-nah)*	
sch *(before e,i)*	sk	Ischia *(ee-skee-ah)*	
sc *(before e,i)*	sh	Scilla *(sheel-lah)*	*Scilla*
sci *(before a,o,u)*	sh	Brescia *(breh-shah)*	
s *(all other cases)*	s	Siena *(see-eh-nah)*	
u	oo	Umbria *(oom-bree-ah)*	
z *(varies)*	ts	Venezia *(veh-neh-tsee-ah)*	
	z	Vicenza *(vee-chehn-zah)*	

Vowels are easy! They are always pronounced the same. "a" is always "ah," "e" is always "eh," "i" is always "ee," "o" is always "oh," and "u" will always be "oo." "h" is never pronounced.

When you arrive in **Italia,** *(ee-tah-lee-ah)* the very first thing you will need to do is to ask questions — "Where is the train station?" "Where can I exchange money?" "Where **(dove)** *(doh-veh)* is the lavatory?" "**Dove** *(doh-veh)* is the restaurant?" "**Dove** *(doh-veh)* do I catch a taxi?" "**Dove** is a good hotel?" "**Dove** is my luggage?" — and the list will go on and on for the entire length of your visit. In Italian, there are SEVEN KEY QUESTION WORDS to learn. For example, the seven key question words will help you find out exactly what you are ordering in a restaurant before you order it — and not after the surprise (or shock!) arrives. Take a few minutes to study and practice saying the seven basic question words listed below. Notice that "what" and "who" are differentiated by only one letter, so be sure not to confuse them. Then cover the Italian words with your hand and fill in each of the blanks with the matching *(pah-roh-lah)(ee-tah-lee-ah-nah)* **parola italiana.**
word   Italian

1. **DOVE** *(doh-veh)* = WHERE   *dove, dove, dove*

2. **CHI** *(kee)* = WHO

3. **CHE** *(keh)* = WHAT

4. **PERCHÈ** *(pehr-keh)* = WHY

5. **QUANDO** *(kwahn-doh)* = WHEN

6. **COME** *(koh-meh)* = HOW

7. **QUANTO** *(kwahn-toh)* = HOW MUCH

3

Now test yourself to see if you really can keep the **parole** *(pah-roh-leh)* straight in your mind. Draw
words

lines between the Italian **e** *(eh)* English equivalents below.
and

why   **chi**

what   **che**

who   **dove**

how   **quanto**

where   **quando**

when   **perchè**

how much   **come**

Examine the following questions containing these **parole.** *(pah-roh-leh)* Practice the sentences many

times **e** *(eh)* then quiz yourself by filling in the blanks below with the correct question **parola.** *(pah-roh-lah)*
and   word

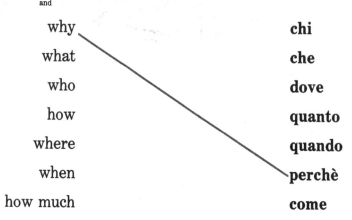

(doh-veh) (eel) (teh-leh-foh-noh)
Dov'è il telefono?
Where is the telephone?

(kee) (eh)
Chi è?
Who is it?

(kwahn-toh) (eh)
Quanto è?
How much is it?

(kwahn-doh) (ahr-ree-vah)(eel) (treh-noh)
Quando arriva il treno?
When does the train arrive?

(keh) (soo-cheh-deh)
Che succede?
What's happening?

(koh-meh) (leen-sah-lah-tah)
Com'è l'insalata?
How is the salad?

(keh) (eh)
Che è?
What is it?

(pehr-keh) (nohn) (ahr-ree-vah)(eel) (seen-yoh-reh)
Perchè non arriva il signore?
Why doesn't arrive the man?

1. _Com'_ è l'insalata?

2. _____ è?

3. _____ succede?

4. _____ è il telefono?

5. _____ non arriva il signore?

6. _____ arriva il treno?

7. _____ è?

8. _____ è?

Dove *(doh-veh)* will be your most used question **parola,** so let's concentrate on it. **Ripeta** *(ree-peh-tah)* the
repeat

following Italian sentences aloud. Then write out each sentence without looking at the

esempio. *(eh-sehm-pee-oh)* If you don't succeed on the first try, don't give up. Just practice each sentence
example

until you are able to do it easily. Don't forget that **"che"** is pronounced like "keh" and

4 **"chi"** like "kee." Also, **"ce"** is pronounced like "cheh" and **"ci"** like "chee."

Dove sono i gabinetti? *(soh-noh)(ee)(gah-bee-net-tee)*

signori | signore

Dov'è il tassì? *(eel) (tahs-see)*

Dov'è l'autobus? *(lah-oo-toh-boos)*

_____   *Dov'è il tassì?*   _____

Dov'è il ristorante? *(eel) (ree-stoh-rahn-teh)*

Dov'è la banca? *(lah) (bahn-kah)*

Dov'è l'albergo? *(lahl-behr-goh)*

Sí, *(see)* many of the **parole** *(pah-roh-leh)* which look like **inglese** *(een-gleh-seh)* are also **italiane.** *(ee-tah-lee-ah-neh)* Since **italiano** *(ee-tah-lee-ah-noh)* **e** *(eh)*
yes   English   Italian

inglese *(een-gleh-seh)* share many words, your work here **è** *(eh)* simpler. You will be amazed at the number
is

of **parole** which are **identiche** *(ee-dehn-tee-keh)* (or almost **identiche**). Of course, they do not always
identical

sound the same when spoken by an Italian, but the **similitudini** *(see-mee-lee-too-dee-nee)* will certainly surprise you.
similarities

Listed below are five "free" **parole** *(pah-roh-leh)* beginning with "a" to help you get started. Be sure to

say each **parola** aloud **e** *(eh)* then write out the **parole italiane** *(ee-tah-lee-ah-neh)* in the blank to the right.

☑ **l'alcool** *(lahl-kohl)* . . . . alcohol
☑ **le Alpi** *(ahl-pee)* . . . . Alps
☑ **americano** *(ah-meh-ree-kah-noh)* . . . . American
☑ **l'animale** *(lah-nee-mah-leh)* . . . . animal
☑ **l'appartamento** *(lahp-pahr-tah-mehn-toh)* . . apartment

_____
_____
l'animale
_____

Free **parole** like these will appear at the bottom of the following pages in a yellow color

band. They are easy — enjoy them!

5

Step 2 "the," "a," "some"

All of these words mean "the" in **italiano**:

(eel)	(loh)	(lah)		(ee)	(l-yee)	(leh)
il	**lo**	**la**	**l'**	**i**	**gli**	**le**

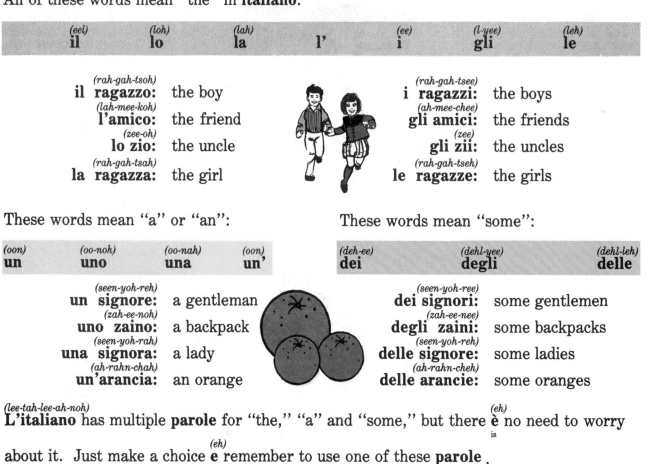

(rah-gah-tsoh)
il ragazzo: the boy

(lah-mee-koh)
l'amico: the friend

(zee-oh)
lo zio: the uncle

(rah-gah-tsah)
la ragazza: the girl

(rah-gah-tsee)
i ragazzi: the boys

(ah-mee-chee)
gli amici: the friends

(zee)
gli zii: the uncles

(rah-gah-tseh)
le ragazze: the girls

These words mean "a" or "an":

(oon)	(oo-noh)	(oo-nah)	(oon)
un	**uno**	**una**	**un'**

(seen-yoh-reh)
un signore: a gentleman

(zah-ee-noh)
uno zaino: a backpack

(seen-yoh-rah)
una signora: a lady

(ah-rahn-chah)
un'arancia: an orange

These words mean "some":

(deh-ee)	(dehl-yee)	(dehl-leh)
dei	**degli**	**delle**

(seen-yoh-ree)
dei signori: some gentlemen

(zah-ee-nee)
degli zaini: some backpacks

(seen-yoh-reh)
delle signore: some ladies

(ah-rahn-cheh)
delle arancie: some oranges

(lee-tah-lee-ah-noh)
L'italiano has multiple **parole** for "the," "a" and "some," but there **è** *(eh)* *is* no need to worry about it. Just make a choice **e** *(eh)* remember to use one of these **parole** .

Step 3

Le Cose *(leh) (koh-seh)*
things

Before you proceed **con** *(kohn)* *with* this Step, situate yourself comfortably in your living room. Now look around you. Can you name the things that you see in the **stanza** *(stahn-zah)* *room* in **italiano**? You can probably guess **la lampada** *(lahm-pah-dah)* and maybe even **il tavolo** *(tah-voh-loh)*. But let's learn the rest of them.

After practicing these **parole** out loud, write them in the blanks below **e** *(eh)* on the next page.

(kwah-droh)
il quadro = the picture _____

(sohf-fee-toh)
il soffitto = the ceiling _____

☐ **l'appetito** *(lahp-peh-tee-toh)* . . . . appetite _____
☐ **aprile** *(ah-pree-leh)* . . . . April _____
☐ **l'arrivo** *(lahr-ree-voh)* . . . . arrival _____
☐ **l'attenzione** *(laht-tehn-tsee-oh-neh)* . . . . . . attention _____
6 ☐ **l'attore** *(laht-toh-reh)* . . . . actor

(lahn-goh-loh)
l'angolo = the corner _____

(fee-neh-strah)
la finestra = the window _____

(lahm-pah-dah)
la lampada = the lamp _____

(loo-cheh)
la luce = the light _____

(soh-fah)
il sofà = the sofa _____

(seh-dee-ah)
la sedia = the chair _____

(tahp-peh-toh)
il tappeto = the carpet _____

(tah-voh-loh)
il tavolo = the table _____

(pohr-tah)
la porta = the door _____

(loh-roh-loh-joh)
l'orologio = the clock _____

(ten-dee-nah)
la tendina = the curtain _____

(pah-reh-teh)
la parete = the wall _____

You will notice that the correct form of **il,** *(eel)* **la** *(oh)* **o l'** is given **con** *(kohn)* each noun. This is for your
with

(een-fohr-mah-tsee-oh-neh)
informazione — just remember to use one of them. Now open your book to the first page
information

con the stick-on labels. Peel off the first 14 labels **e** *(eh)* proceed around the **stanza,** *(stahn-zah)*
room

labeling these items in your home. This will help to increase your Italian **parola** power

easily. Don't forget to say **le parole** as you attach each label.

Now ask yourself, **"Dov'è il** *(eel)* **quadro?"** **e** point at it while you answer, **"Ecco** *(ehk-koh)* **il quadro."** *(kwah-droh)*
there is

Continue on down the **lista** *(lee-stah)* until you feel comfortable with these new **parole.** Say,
list

"Dov'è *(eel)* **il soffitto?"** *(sohf-fee-toh)* Then **risponda,** *(ree-spohn-dah)* **"Ecco il soffitto,"** and so on. When you
respond

identify all the items on the **lista,** *(lee-stah)* you will be ready to move on.

Now, starting on the next page, let's learn some basic parts of the house.

☐ **la baia** *(bah-ee-ah)* .... bay _____
☐ **il balcone** *(bahl-koh-neh)* .... balcony _____
☐ **la banana** *(bah-nah-nah)* .... banana _____
☐ **la banca** *(bahn-kah)* .... bank _____
☐ **la benedizione** *(beh-neh-dee-tsee-oh-neh)* .... benediction _____

7

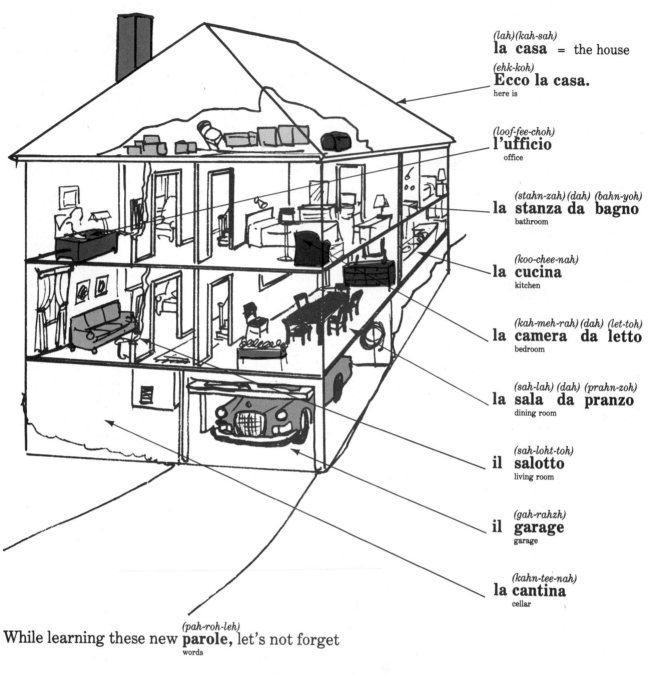

(lah) (kah-sah)
la casa = the house

(ehk-koh)
Ecco la casa.
here is

(loof-fee-choh)
l'ufficio
office

(stahn-zah) (dah) (bahn-yoh)
la stanza da bagno
bathroom

(koo-chee-nah)
la cucina
kitchen

(kah-meh-rah) (dah) (let-toh)
la camera da letto
bedroom

(sah-lah) (dah) (prahn-zoh)
la sala da pranzo
dining room

(sah-loht-toh)
il salotto
living room

(gah-rahzh)
il garage
garage

(kahn-tee-nah)
la cantina
cellar

(pah-roh-leh)
While learning these new **parole,** let's not forget
words

(lah-oo-toh) (mahk-kee-nah)
l'auto/la macchina

(bee-chee-klet-tah)
la bicicletta

(kah-neh)
il cane

il cane

☐ **il biscotto** *(bee-skoht-toh)*	biscuit, cookie
☐ **la bistecca** *(bee-stehk-kah)*	beefsteak
☐ **la bottiglia** *(boht-teel-yah)*	bottle
☐ **breve** *(breh-veh)*	brief, short
☐ **brillante** *(breel-lahn-teh)*	brilliant, shining

(gaht-toh)
il gatto

(jahr-dee-noh)
il giardino

(poh-stah)
la posta

il giardino

_____

(boo-kah) (del-leh) (let-teh-reh)
la buca delle lettere

(fee-oh-ree)
i fiori

(kahm-pah-nel-loh)
il campanello
doorbell

_____

Peel off the next set of labels *(eh)* **e** wander through your *(kah-sah)* **casa** learning these new *(pah-roh-leh)* **parole.**

Granted, it will be somewhat difficult to label your *(kah-neh) (gaht-toh)* *(fee-oh-ree)* **cane, gatto o fiori,** but use your

(eem-mah-jee-nah-tsee-oh-neh)
immaginazione.

Again, practice by asking yourself, **"Dov'è il** *(jahr-dee-noh)* **giardino?"** *(ree-spohn-dah)* **e risponda, "Ecco il giardino."**

Dov'è...

☐ **la capitale** *(kah-pee-tah-leh)* .... capital _____
☐ **il castello** *(kah-stehl-loh)* .... castle _____
☐ **la categoria** *(kah-teh-goh-ree-ah)* .... category _____
☐ **la cattedrale** *(kaht-teh-drah-leh)* .... cathedral _____
☐ **il centro** *(chehn-troh)* .... center, downtown _____

9

Step 4

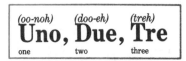

(oo-noh) *(doo-eh)* *(treh)*
Uno, Due, Tre
one   two   three

(bahm-bee-nee) (ee-tah-lee-ah-nee)
You might hear **bambini italiani** reciting this rhyme:
           children   Italian

(lah) (pehp-pee-nah) (fah)   (eel) (kahf-feh)
Uno, due, tre, la Peppina fa il caffè;
one   two   three   Peppina   makes the coffee

(kwaht-troh)   (cheen-kweh) (seh-ee) (ahnk-ee-oh) (loh) (vohr-reh-ee)
Quattro, cinque, sei, anch'io lo vorrei.
four   five   six   also   I   it   would like

For some reason, numbers are not the easiest thing to learn, but just remember how

(kohn-vehr-sah-tsee-oh-neh)
important they are in everyday **conversazione.** How could you tell someone your phone
                       conversation

number, your address or your hotel room if you had no numbers? And think of how

difficult it would be if you could not understand the time, the price of an apple or the

(ah-oo-toh-boos)   *(noo-meh-ree)*   *(see-mee-lee-too-dee-nee)*
correct **autobus** to take. When practicing the **numeri** below, notice the **similitudini**
bus   numbers   similarities

(kwaht-troh)   *(kwaht-tohr-dee-chee)*   *(set-teh)*   *(dee-chahs-set-teh)*
between **quattro** (4) and **quattordici** (14), **sette** (7) and **diciassette** (17) **e** so on.

#		#	
0	*(zeh-roh)* **zero**		
1	*(oo-noh)* **uno**	11	*(oon-dee-chee)* **undici**
2	*(doo-eh)* **due**	12	*(doh-dee-chee)* **dodici**
3	*(treh)* **tre**	13	*(treh-dee-chee)* **tredici**
4	*(kwaht-troh)* **quattro**	14	*(kwaht-tohr-dee-chee)* **quattordici**
5	*(cheen-kweh)* **cinque**	15	*(kween-dee-chee)* **quindici**
6	*(seh-ee)* **sei**	16	*(seh-dee-chee)* **sedici**
7	*(set-teh)* **sette**	17	*(dee-chahs-set-teh)* **diciassette**
8	*(oht-toh)* **otto**	18	*(dee-choht-toh)* **diciotto**
9	*(noh-veh)* **nove**	19	*(dee-chahn-noh-veh)* **diciannove**
10	*(dee-eh-chee)* **dieci**	20	*(ven-tee)* **venti**

0   *zero, zero, zero* _____
1 _____
2 _____
3 _____
4 _____
5 _____
6 _____
7 _____
8 _____
9 _____
10 _____

☐ **la cerimonia** *(cheh-ree-moh-nee-ah)* .... ceremony   _____
☐ **certo** *(chehr-toh)* .... certainly   _____
☐ **il cinema** *(chee-neh-mah)* .... cinema, movie house   _____
☐ **il cioccolato** *(chok-koh-lah-toh)* .... chocolate   _____
☐ **la comunicazione** *(koh-moo-nee-kah-tsee-oh-neh)* communication   _____

(oo-see) **Usi** these *(noo-meh-ree)* **numeri** on a daily basis. Count to yourself *(een)* **in italiano** when you brush your
use

teeth, exercise, *(oh)* **o** commute to work. Now fill in the following blanks according to the
or

numeri in parentheses.

Note: This is a good time to start learning these two important phrases.

(vohr-reh-ee) **vorrei**	=	I would like _____
(vohr-rehm-moh) **vorremmo**	=	we would like _____

(vohr-reh-ee) **Vorrei** _____ (15) *(fohl-yee)(dee) (kahr-tah)* **fogli di carta.** pieces of paper   **Quanti?** _____ (15)

Vorrei _____ (10) *(kahr-toh-lee-neh)* **cartoline.** postcards   **Quanti?** _____ (10)

Vorrei _____ (11) *(frahn-koh-bohl-lee)* **francobolli.** stamps   **Quanti?** _____ (11)

Vorrei _____ (8) *(lee-tree)(dee) (behn-zee-nah)* **litri di benzina.** liters of gasoline   **Quanti?** _otto_ (8)

Vorrei _____ (1) *(beek-kee-eh-reh)(dee) (ah-rahn-chah-tah)* **bicchiere di aranciata.** glass of orangeade   **Quanti?** _____ (1)

(vohr-rehm-moh) **Vorremmo** _____ (3) *(beel-yet-tee) (ah-oo-toh-boos)* **biglietti dell'autobus** bus tickets   **Quanti?** _____ (3)

Vorremmo _____ (4) *(tah-tseh) (dee) (teh)* **tazze di tè.** cups of tea   **Quanti?** _____ (4)

Vorremmo _due_ (2) *(beer-reh)* **birre.** beers   **Quanti?** _____ (2)

Vorrei _____ (12) *(oo-oh-vah)(freh-skeh)* **uova fresche.** eggs fresh   **Quanti?** _____ (12)

Vorremmo _____ (6) *(kee-lee) (dee) (kahr-neh)* **chili di carne.** kilos of meat   **Quanti?** _____ (6)

Vorremmo _____ (5) *(beek-kee-eh-ree) (dee) (vee-noh)* **bicchieri di vino.** glasses of wine   **Quanti?** _____ (5)

Vorrei _____ (7) *(beek-kee-eh-ree) (dee) (ahk-kwah)* **bicchieri di acqua.** glasses of water   **Quanti?** _____ (7)

Vorremmo _____ (9) *(kee-lee) (dee) (boor-roh)* **chili di burro.** kilos of butter   **Quanti?** _____ (9)

☐ **la conservazione** *(kohn-sehr-vah-tsee-oh-neh)* . conservation _____
☐ **la conversazione** *(kohn-vehr-sah-tsee-oh-neh)* . conversation _____
☐ **il coraggio** *(koh-rah-joh)* .... courage _____
☐ **la cugina** *(koo-jee-nah)* .... female cousin _____
☐ **il cugino** *(koo-jee-noh)* .... male cousin _____

Now see if you can translate the following thoughts into **italiano**. **Le** *(leh)* **risposte** *(ree-spoh-steh)* are

answers

at the bottom of the **pagina.** *(pah-jee-nah)*

page

1. I would like seven postcards.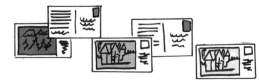

_____

2. I would like one beer. *Vorrei una birra.*

3. We would like two glasses of water.

_____

4. We would like three bus tickets.

_____

Review **i numeri** 1 **a** *(ah)* 20 **e** answer the following **domande** *(doh-mahn-deh)* aloud, **e** then write the

to   questions

risposte *(ree-spoh-steh)* in the blank spaces to the left.

Quanti tavoli *(kwahn-tee) (tah-voh-lee)* **ci sono?** *(chee)(soh-noh)*   *tre*

how many   there are

Quante lampade *(lahm-pah-deh)*

ci sono? *(chee)(soh-noh)*   _____

Quante sedie ci sono? *(seh-dee-eh)*   _____

12

(kwahn-tee) (oh-roh-loh-jee)(chee) (soh-noh)
Quanti orologi ci sono?
how many

_____

(fee-neh-streh)
Quante finestre ci sono?

uno

(pehr-soh-neh)
Quante persone ci sono?

_____

(seen-yoh-ree)
Quanti signori ci sono?
men

_____

(dohn-neh)
Quante donne ci sono?
women

| (koh-loh-ree) |
| **I Colori** |
| colors |

Step 5

(ee) (koh-loh-ree)(soh-noh)   (een) (ee-tah-lee-ah)   (ah-meh-ree-kah)   (noh-mee)
I colori sono the same **in Italia** as **in America** — they just have different **nomi.**
are   names

(vee-oh-leht-toh)   (kah-sah)
You can easily recognize **violetto** as violet. So when you are invited to someone's **casa**
house

(kohr-reht-toh)
e you want to bring flowers, you will be able to order the **colore corretto** of flowers.

(een) (eh-oo-roh-pah)(fee-oh-ree)(rohs-see)   (roh-seh) (rohs-seh)
(Contrary to American custom, **in Europa i fiori rossi, e** particularly **le rose rosse,**
red   roses   red

are only exchanged between lovers!) Let's learn the basic **colori.** Once you have read through

(lee-stah)   (pah-jee-nah)   (mah-noh)
la lista on the next **pagina,** cover the **italiano con** your **mano, e** practice writing out the
with   hand

(ee-tah-lee-ah-noh)   (een-gleh-seh)   (see-mee-lee-too-dee-nee)
italiano next to the **inglese.** Notice the **similitudini** between **le parole in italiano e**

in inglese.

☐ **la danza** *(dahn-tsah)* . . . . dance   _____
☐ **decorato** *(deh-koh-rah-toh)* . . . . decorated   _____
☐ **delizioso** *(deh-lee-tsee-oh-soh)* . . . . delicious
☐ **denso** *(dehn-soh)* . . . . dense   _____
☐ **il desiderio** *(deh-see-deh-ree-oh)* . . . . desire   _____

13

(bee-ahn-koh)
bianco = white_____

(bahr-kah) (eh)(bee-ahn-kah)
La barca è bianca.
boat   is

(neh-roh)
nero = black_____

(pahl-lah) (neh-rah)
La palla è nera.
ball

(jahl-loh)
giallo = yellow_____

(bah-nah-nah) (jahl-lah)
La banana è gialla.

(rohs-soh)
rosso = red_____

(lee-broh)
Il libro è rosso.
book

(ah-zoor-roh)
azzurro = blue *azzurro*_____

(mahk-kee-nah) (ah-zoor-rah)
La macchina è azzurra.
car

(gree-joh)
grigio = gray_____

(leh-leh-fahn-teh)
L'elefante è grigio.

(mahr-roh-neh)
marrone = brown_____

(seh-dee-ah)
La sedia è marrone.
chair

(vehr-deh)
verde = green_____

(lehr-bah)
L'erba è verde.
grass

(roh-sah)
rosa = pink_____

(fee-oh-reh)
Il fiore è rosa.
flower

(mool-tee-koh-loh-reh)
multicolore = multi-colored_____

(lahm-pah-dah)
La lampada è multicolore.

(dee-eh-chee)
Now peel off the next **dieci** labels **e** proceed to label these *(koh-loh-ree)* **colori** in your *(kah-sah)* **casa**.

Now let's practice using these **parole**.

(bee-ahn-kah)
Dov'è la barca bianca?

(ehk-koh)
Ecco la barca *bianca*.
there is

(gree-joh)
Dov'è il tavolo grigio?

Ecco il tavolo _____.

(mahr-roh-neh)
Dov'è la sedia marrone?

Ecco la sedia _____.

(bee-ahn-kah)
Dov'è la palla bianca?

Ecco la palla _____.

Dov'è la lampada multicolore?

Ecco la lampada _____.

(rohs-soh)
Dov'è il libro rosso?

Ecco il libro _____.

☐ **dicembre** *(dee-chem-breh)*	December	_____
☐ **diretto** *(dee-reht-toh)*	direct	_____
☐ **il disastro** *(dee-sah-stroh)*	disaster, accident	_____
☐ **la distanza** *(dee-stahn-tsah)*	distance	_____
☐ **divino** *(dee-vee-noh)*	divine	_____

14

Dov'è la porta *(vehr-deh)* verde?   Ecco la porta _____.

Dov'è la casa *(roh-sah)* rosa?   Ecco la casa _____.

Dov'è la banana *(jahl-lah)* gialla?   Ecco la banana _____.

Note: **In *(een)* italiano,** the **verbo *(vehr-boh)*** for "to have" **è "avere,"** *(ah-veh-reh)* which looks like...

ho *(oh)* = I have _____   **abbiamo *(ahb-bee-ah-moh)*** = we have _____

Let's review **"vorrei"** *(vohr-reh-ee)* (would like) e learn **"ho"** *(oh)* (I have) and **"abbiamo."** *(ahb-bee-ah-moh)* (we have) **Ripeta** *(ree-peh-tah)* each sentence out loud.

Vorrei un bicchiere di birra. *(vohr-reh-ee)(oon)(beek-kee-eh-reh)(dee)(beer-rah)* (glass)   **Ho un bicchiere di birra.** *(oh)*

Vorremmo *(vohr-rehm-moh)* **due bicchieri di vino.** *(vee-noh)*   **Abbiamo due bicchieri di vino.** *(ahb-bee-ah-moh)*

Vorrei un bicchiere di acqua. *(ahk-kwah)*   **Abbiamo una casa.** *(oo-nah)*

Vorremmo un'insalata. *(oo-neen-sah-lah-tah)*   **Ho una casa in America.** *(een)(ah-meh-ree-kah)*

Vorremmo avere una macchina. *(ah-veh-reh)(mahk-kee-nah)*   **Ho una macchina.** *(mahk-kee-nah)*

Vorremmo avere una macchina in Europa. *(eh-oo-roh-pah)*   **Abbiamo una macchina in Europa.**

Now fill in the following blanks **con the forma corretta** *(fohr-mah)(kohr-ret-tah)* (form) (correct) of "avere" **o "vorrei."** *(oh)(voh-reh-ee)* (or)

Abbiamo _____ tre macchine.
(we have)

_____ due biglietti dell'autobus.
(we would like)

_____ un quadro.
(I have)

_____ sette cartoline.
(I would like)

☐ **il dizionario** *(dee-tsee-oh-nah-ree-oh)* ...... dictionary
☐ **il dollaro** *(dohl-lah-roh)* .... dollar
☐ **il dottore** *(doht-toh-reh)* .... doctor
☐ **il dubbio** *(doob-bee-oh)* .... doubt
☐ **durante** *(doo-rahn-teh)* .... during

_____
_____
_____
_____

15

Ecco a quick review of the *(koh-loh-ree)* **colori.** Draw lines between **le parole italiane e i** *(leh) (pah-roh-leh)* *(eh) (ee)*
and the

(kohr-ret-tee)
colori corretti.

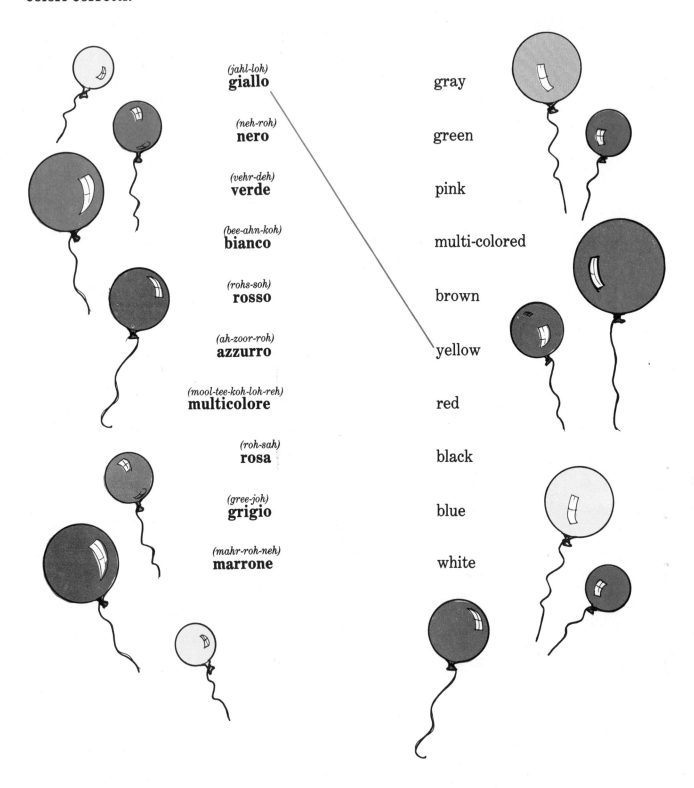

(jahl-loh)
giallo

(neh-roh)
nero

(vehr-deh)
verde

(bee-ahn-koh)
bianco

(rohs-soh)
rosso

(ah-zoor-roh)
azzurro

(mool-tee-koh-loh-reh)
multicolore

(roh-sah)
rosa

(gree-joh)
grigio

(mahr-roh-neh)
marrone

gray

green

pink

multi-colored

brown

yellow

red

black

blue

white

□ **eccellente** *(eh-chehl-len-teh)* . . . . excellent
□ **l'economia** *(leh-koh-noh-mee-ah)* . . . . economy
□ **l'entrata** *(len-trah-tah)* . . . . entrance
□ **est** *(ehst)* . . . . east
16 □ **Europa** *(eh-oo-roh-pah)* . . . . Europe

(eel) (deh-nah-roh)
Il Denaro
money

Before starting this Step, go back **e** review Step 4. Make sure you can count to *(ven-tee)* **venti** without looking back at **il libro** *(lee-broh)*. Let's learn the larger **numeri** *(noo-meh-ree)* now, as you will hardly find anything that costs less than 20 **lire** *(lee-reh)*. After practicing aloud **i numeri italiani** 10 **a** *(ah)* 100 below, write these **numeri** in the blanks provided. Again, notice the *to* **similitudini** *(see-mee-lee-too-dee-nee)* between **numeri** such as **quattro** *(kwaht-troh)* (4), **quattordici** *(kwaht-tohr-dee-chee)* (14) and **quaranta** *(kwah-rahn-tah)* (40).

10	**dieci** *(dee-eh-chee)*	(quattro + sei = dieci)	10	*dieci, dieci, dieci*
20	**venti** *(ven-tee)*	(due = 2)	20	
30	**trenta** *(tren-tah)*	(tre = 3)	30	
40	**quaranta** *(kwah-rahn-tah)*	(quattro = 4)	40	
50	**cinquanta** *(cheen-kwahn-tah)*	(cinque = 5)	50	
60	**sessanta** *(sehs-sahn-tah)*	(sei = 6)	60	
70	**settanta** *(set-tahn-tah)*	(sette = 7)	70	
80	**ottanta** *(oht-tahn-tah)*	(otto = 8)	80	
90	**novanta** *(noh-vahn-tah)*	(nove = 9)	90	
100	**cento** *(chen-toh)*		100	
1000	**mille** *(meel-leh)*		1000	
2000	**due mila** *(doo-eh) (mee-lah)*		2000	

Now take a logical guess. **Come** *(koh-meh)* would you write (**e** say) the following? **Le risposte** *(ree-spoh-steh)* **sono** *(soh-noh)* at the bottom of **la pagina** *(lah) (pah-jee-nah)*.
are

400 _____   600 _____

2000 _____   5300 _____

The unit of currency **in Italia è la lira** *(lee-rah)* **italiana,** *(ee-tah-lee-ah-nah)* abbreviated **£.** Bills are called **biglietti** *(beel-yet-tee)* and coins are called **monete.** *(moh-neh-teh)* The **lira** is the only monetary unit **in Italia** and can not be broken down into smaller units. You will find that hundreds of **lire** *(lee-reh)* are equivalent to an American **dollaro,** *(dohl-lah-roh)* so you will want to become very familiar with large numbers.

Always be sure to practice each **parola** out loud. You might want to exchange some money **adesso** *(ah-dehs-soh)* so that you can familiarize yourself **con** the various types of **denaro.** *(deh-nah-roh)*
now   money

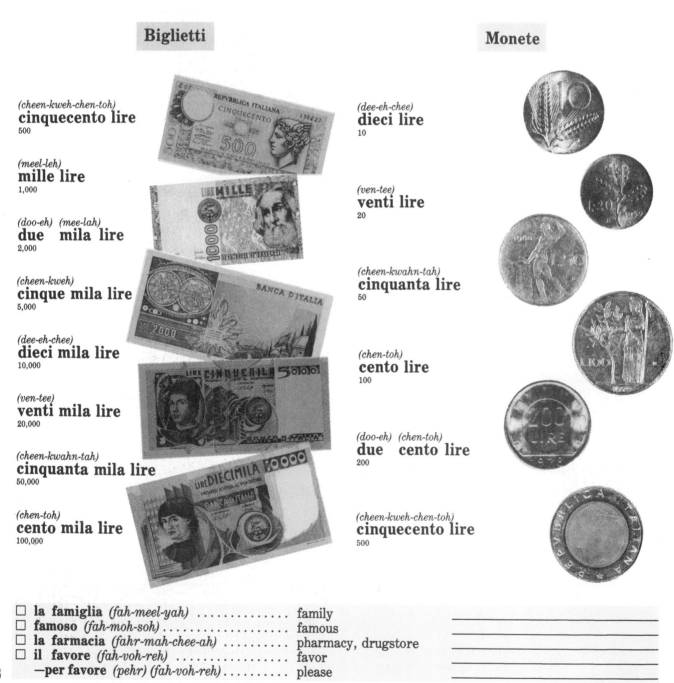

Biglietti

cinquecento lire *(cheen-kweh-chen-toh)*
500

mille lire *(meel-leh)*
1,000

due mila lire *(doo-eh) (mee-lah)*
2,000

cinque mila lire *(cheen-kweh)*
5,000

dieci mila lire *(dee-eh-chee)*
10,000

venti mila lire *(ven-tee)*
20,000

cinquanta mila lire *(cheen-kwahn-tah)*
50,000

cento mila lire *(chen-toh)*
100,000

Monete

dieci lire *(dee-eh-chee)*
10

venti lire *(ven-tee)*
20

cinquanta lire *(cheen-kwahn-tah)*
50

cento lire *(chen-toh)*
100

due cento lire *(doo-eh) (chen-toh)*
200

cinquecento lire *(cheen-kweh-chen-toh)*
500

☐ **la famiglia** *(fah-meel-yah)* .... family
☐ **famoso** *(fah-moh-soh)* .... famous
☐ **la farmacia** *(fahr-mah-chee-ah)* .... pharmacy, drugstore
☐ **il favore** *(fah-voh-reh)* .... favor
  —**per favore** *(pehr) (fah-voh-reh)* .... please

Review **i numeri dieci** through **mille** again. **Adesso,** *(ah-dehs-soh)* how do you say "twenty-two"

o *(oh)* "fifty-three" *(een)* **in italiano?** You basically put **i numeri** together in a logical sequence:

for example, 62 (60 + 2) is **sessantadue.** See if you can say **e** write **i numeri** on this

pagina. **Le risposte sono** *(soh-noh)* at the bottom of **la pagina.**

a. 25 = _____
(20 + 5)

b. 47 = _____
(40 + 7)

c. 84 = _____
(80 + 4)

d. 51 = _____
(50 + 1)

e. 36 = _____
(30 + 6)

f. 93 = _____
(90 + 3)

g. 68 = *sessantotto*
(60 + 8)

h. 72 = _____
(70 + 2)

To ask what something costs **in italiano,** one asks, **"Quanto costa?"** *(kwahn-toh) (koh-stah)*

Adesso *(ah-dehs-soh)* answer the following questions based on **i numeri** in parentheses.

1. **Quanto costa?** *(kwahn-toh) (koh-stah)*

Costa *(koh-stah)* *dieci* **lire.** *(lee-reh)*
(10)

2. **Quanto costa?**

Costa _____ **lire.**
(20)

3. **Quanto costa il libro?** *(lee-broh)*

Costa _____ **lire.**
(17)

4. **Quanto costa l'auto?** *(lah-oo-toh)*

Costa _____ **lire.**
(90,000)

5. **Quanto costa il film?** *(feelm)*

Costa _____ **lire.**
(3,000)

6. **Quanto costa la camera?** *(kah-meh-rah)* room

Costa _____ **lire.**
(15,000)

7. **Quanto costa il quadro?** *(kwah-droh)*

Costa _____ **lire.**
(100,000)

RISPOSTE

7. cento mila	2. venti	e. trentasei
6. quindici mila	1. dieci	d. cinquantuno
5. tre mila	h. settantadue	c. ottantaquattro
4. novanta mila	g. sessantotto	b. quarantasette
3. diciassette	f. novantatré	a. venticinque

19

Step 7

(oh-jee) **(doh-mah-nee)** **(ee-eh-ree)**
Oggi, Domani, e Ieri
today   tomorrow   yesterday

(kah-len-dah-ree-oh) **Il calendario** calendar						
(set-tee-mah-nah) **Una settimana** *(ah)* **ha sette** *(johr-nee)* **giorni.** week — has — days						
(loo-neh-dee) **lunedì**	*(mahr-teh-dee)* **martedì**	*(mehr-koh-leh-dee)* **mercoledì**	*(joh-veh-dee)* **giovedì**	*(veh-nehr-dee)* **venerdì**	*(sah-bah-toh)* **sabato**	*(doh-meh-nee-kah)* **domenica**
1	2	3	4	5	6	7

(mohl-toh) *(eem-pohr-tahn-teh)*
È molto importante to know the days of the week **e** the various parts of the day.
it is very   important

Let's learn them. Be sure to say them aloud before filling in the blanks below.

(l-yee)(ee-tah-lee-ah-nee) *(set-tee-mah-nah)* *(loo-neh-dee)*
Gli Italiani begin counting their **settimana** on Monday with **lunedì.**
the Italians week

(loo-neh-dee)
lunedì _lunedì_   *(mahr-teh-dee)* **martedì** _____
Monday   Tuesday

(mehr-koh-leh-dee)
mercoledì _____   *(joh-veh-dee)* **giovedì** _____
Wednesday   Thursday

(veh-nehr-dee)
venerdì _____   *(sah-bah-toh)* **sabato** _____
Friday   Saturday

(doh-meh-nee-kah)
domenica _____
Sunday

(oh-jee) *(doh-mah-nee)* *(ee-eh-ree)* *(eh-rah)*
If **oggi è mercoledì**, then **domani è giovedì e ieri era martedì.** **Adesso,** you supply
today   tomorrow   yesterday was

le risposte corrette. If **oggi è lunedì**, then **domani è** _____ **e ieri era**

_____. **O,** if **oggi è lunedì**, then _____ **è martedì e** _ieri_

era domenica. *(keh)* *(johr-noh)* **Che giorno è oggi? Oggi è** _____.
what day is

(ah-dehs-soh) *(set-teh)* *(kah-len-dah-ree-oh)*
Adesso, peel off the next **sette** labels **e** put them on a **calendario** you use every day.

(oh-jee)
From **oggi** on, Monday **è "lunedì."**

☐ **il filtro** *(feel-troh)*	filter	_____
☐ **finalmente** *(fee-nahl-mehn-teh)*	finally	_____
☐ **finito** *(fee-nee-toh)*	finished, ended	_____
☐ **la fontana** *(fohn-tah-nah)*	fountain	_____
☐ **la forchetta** *(fohr-keht-tah)*	fork	_____

20

There are **quattro** *(kwaht-troh)* parts to each **giorno** *(johr-noh)*.
day

morning = **mattina** *(maht-tee-nah)*	_____
afternoon = **pomeriggio** *(poh-meh-ree-joh)*	_____
evening = **sera** *(seh-rah)*	*sera, sera, sera, sera, sera*
night = **notte** *(noht-teh)*	_____

Notice that the Italian days of the **settimana** *(set-tee-mah-nah)* are not capitalized as **in inglese**. **Adesso** *(ah-dehs-soh)*,
week

fill in the following blanks **e** then check your **risposte** at the bottom of **la pagina**.

a. Sunday morning = *domenica mattina*

b. Friday evening = _____

c. Saturday evening = _____

d. Monday morning = _____

e. Wednesday morning = _____

f. Tuesday afternoon = _____

g. Thursday afternoon = _____

h. Thursday evening = _____

i. yesterday evening = _____

j. yesterday morning = _____

k. tomorrow evening = _____

l. tomorrow afternoon = _____

m. yesterday afternoon = _____

21

So, **con** merely **undici parole**, _(kohn)_ _(oon-dee-chee)_ you can specify any day of the **settimana e** _(set-tee-mah-nah)_ any time of the

giorno. _(johr-noh)_ Le parole "**oggi**," _(oh-jee)_ "**domani**" e "**ieri**" _(ee-eh-ree)_ will be **molto** _(mohl-toh)_ **importanti** _(eem-pohr-tahn-tee)_ for you in
very

making **prenotazioni** _(preh-noh-tah-tsee-oh-nee)_ e **appuntamenti,** _(ahp-poon-tah-men-tee)_ in getting **biglietti** _(beel-yet-tee)_ **teatrali** _(teh-ah-trah-lee)_ e many things you will
reservations   appointments   theater tickets

want to do. Knowing the parts of **il giorno** will help you to learn e understand the various

saluti _(sah-loo-tee)_ **italiani** _(ee-tah-lee-ah-nee)_ below. Practice these every day now until your trip.
greetings

good morning good afternoon	=	**buon giorno** _(bwohn)_ _(johr-noh)_
good evening	=	**buona sera** _(bwoh-nah)_ _(seh-rah)_
good night	=	**buona notte** _(bwoh-nah)_ _(noht-teh)_
hi!/bye!	=	**ciao** _(chah-oh)_
How are you?	=	**Come va?** _(koh-meh)_ _(vah)_

buona notte

Take the next **quattro** labels e stick them on the appropriate **cose** _(koh-seh)_ in your **casa.** _(kah-sah)_
things

How about the bathroom mirror **per** _(pehr)_ "**buon giorno**"? O the front door **per "buona sera"**?
for

O your alarm clock **per "buona notte"**? Remember that, whenever you enter small shops

e stores **in Italia,** you will hear the appropriate **saluto** _(sah-loo-toh)_ for the time of day. Don't be
greeting

surprised. It is a **molto** _(mohl-toh)_ friendly e warm **costume.** _(koh-stoo-meh)_ Everyone greets everyone e you should
very   custom

too, if you really want to enjoy **l'Italia.** You **è** about one-fourth of your way through **il libro** _(lee-broh)_

ed è _(ed)_ _(eh)_ a good time to quickly review **le parole** you have learned before doing the crossword

puzzle on the next **pagina.** **Buon** _(bwohn)_ **divertimento** _(dee-vehr-tee-men-toh)_ e **buona** _(bwoh-nah)_ **fortuna.** _(for-too-nah)_
have fun   good   luck

RISPOSTE TO CROSSWORD PUZZLE (PAROLE CROCIATE)

ACROSS

1. vorrei
2. parete
3. grigio
4. signore
5. luce
6. pittura
7. domenica
8. con
9. moneta
10. cinque
11. denaro
12. nero
13. giallo
14. chi
15. giorno

16. risposta
17. avere
18. orologio
19. tre
21. quanto
22. multicolore
23. sera
24. oggi
25. perché
26. notte
27. ecco
28. abbiamo

DOWN

1. venerdì
2. ieri
3. angolo
4. sedia
5. sabato
6. diciannove
7. pomeriggio
8. acqua
9. banca
10. cartolina
11. donna
13. ciao
14. che è
15. soffitto
16. verde

17. bianco
19. tendina
20. lampada
21. quattro
22. martedì
23. due
24. rosso
25. come

22

CROSSWORD PUZZLE (PAROLE CROCIATE)
(kroh-chah-teh)

ACROSS

1. I would like
2. wall
3. gray
4. gentleman
5. light
6. paint
7. Sunday
8. with
9. coin
10. five
11. money
12. black
13. yellow
14. who
15. day
16. answer
17. to have
18. clock
19. three
21. how much
22. multi-colored
23. evening
24. today
25. why
26. night
27. there is/are
28. we have

DOWN

1. Friday
2. yesterday
3. corner
4. chair
5. Saturday
6. nineteen
7. afternoon
8. water
9. bank
10. postcard
11. woman
13. hi!/bye!
14. what is
15. ceiling
16. green
17. white
19. curtain
20. lamp
21. four
22. Tuesday
23. two
24. red
25. how

23

Step 8

> *(een)* *(soh-prah)* *(soht-toh)*
> # In, Sopra, Sotto . . .
> in   over   under

(preh-poh-see-tsee-oh-nee)
Le preposizioni italiane (words like "in," "on," "through" and "next to") **sono** very
_{are}

useful **e** they allow you to be precise **con** a minimum of effort. Instead of having to point

(seh-ee)
sei times at a piece of yummy pastry you wish to order, you can explain precisely which

(eh)
one you want by saying **è** behind, in front of, next to, **o** under the piece of the pastry
_{it is}

(peek-koh-leh)
the salesperson is starting to pick up. Let's learn some of these **piccole parole** which
_{little}

(mohl-toh)(see-mee-lee)   *(eh-sem-pee)*
sono molto simili to **inglese.** Study the **esempi** below.
_{similar}   _{examples}

(dah)   *(dahl)* *(dahl-lah)*
da (often seen as **dal, dalla,** etc.) = of/from   *(ahk-kahn-toh)* *(ah)*   *(soht-toh)*
_{from the}   **accanto a** = next to   **sotto** = under
(een)   *(nel)* *(nel-lah)*
in (often seen as **nel, nella,** etc.) = into/in   *(soh-prah)*
                                                                                      sopra = over

---

(ehn-trah) *(nel)* *(noo-oh-voh)(ahl-behr-goh)*
Il signore entra nel nuovo albergo.
_{enters} _{in the} _{new} _{hotel}

(dohn-nah) *(vee-eh-neh)* *(dahl)* *(eh-chel-len-teh)*
La donna viene dall'eccellente albergo.
_{woman} _{comes} _{from the excellent}

(meh-dee-koh) *(bwohn)*
Il medico è nel buon albergo.
_{physician} _{good}

(soh-prah) *(tah-voh-loh)*
Il nuovo quadro è sopra il tavolo.
_{table}
(ahk-kahn-toh) *(oh-roh-loh-joh)*
Il nuovo quadro è accanto all'orologio.
_{clock}

(kah-neh) *(soht-toh)*
Il cane grigio è sotto il tavolo marrone.
_{dog}

Il tavolo marrone è sopra il cane.

L'orologio verde è sopra il tavolo.

L'orologio verde è accanto al quadro.

☐ **la foresta** *(foh-reh-stah)* . . . . forest _____
☐ **la forma** *(fohr-mah)* . . . . form _____
☐ **Francia** *(frahn-chah)* . . . . France _____
☐ **fresco** *(freh-skoh)* . . . . cool, fresh _____
24 ☐ **la frutta** *(froot-tah)* . . . . fruit _____

Fill in the blanks below **con le preposizioni corrette** *(preh-poh-see-tsee-oh-nee)* according to the **illustrazioni** *(eel-loo-strah-tsee-oh-nee)* on the previous **pagina**.

pictures

Il signore entra _____ **nuovo albergo.** *(ahl-behr-goh)*

Il cane grigio è _*sotto*_ **il tavolo.**

L'orologio verde è _____ **il tavolo.** *(loh-roh-loh-joh)* *(tah-voh-loh)*

Il medico è _____ **buon albergo.**

L'orologio verde è _____ **al quadro.**

Il nuovo quadro è _____ **il tavolo.**

Il tavolo marrone è _____ **il quadro.**

Il nuovo quadro è _____ **all'orologio.**

La donna viene _____ **eccellente albergo.** *(eh-chel-len-teh)*

Il tavolo marrone è _____ **l'orologio.**

Adesso, risponda alle domande based on le illustrazioni on the previous pagina.
(ah-dehs-soh) *(doh-mahn-deh)* *(eel-loo-strah-tsee-oh-nee)*
to the questions

(doh-veh) *(eel)*
Dov'è il medico? _____

Dov'è il cane? *(kah-neh)* _____

Dov'è il tavolo? _____

Dov'è il quadro? _____

(keh) *(fah)*
Che fa la donna? _____
does

(keh) *(fah)*
Che fa il signore? _____
does

È verde l'orologio? _*Sì, l'orologio è verde.*_
is

È grigio il cane? _*Sì,*_ _____
is

☐ **la galleria** *(gahl-leh-ree-ah)* .... gallery
☐ **gennaio** *(jehn-nah-ee-oh)* .... January
☐ **gentile** *(jehn-tee-leh)* .... gentle, kind
☐ **la geografia** *(jeh-oh-grah-fee-ah)* .... geography
☐ **la giacca** *(jahk-kah)* .... jacket

_____
_____
_____
_____
_____ 25

Adesso for some more practice **con le preposizioni italiane.**

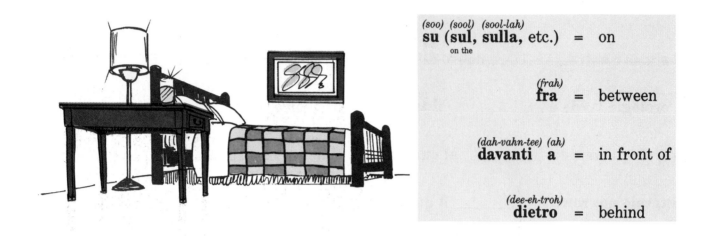

(soo) (sool) (sool-lah)
su (sul, sulla, etc.) = on
on the

(frah)
fra = between

(dah-vahn-tee) (ah)
davanti a = in front of

(dee-eh-troh)
dietro = behind

(beek-kee-eh-reh) (dee) (ahk-kwah) (sool)
Il bicchiere di acqua è sul tavolo.
of · on the

Il bicchiere di acqua è _____ **tavolo.**

(dee-eh-troh)
Il letto è dietro il tavolo.

Il letto è ___*dietro*___ **il tavolo.**

La lampada gialla è dietro il tavolo.

La lampada gialla è _____ **il tavolo.**

(dah-vahn-tee)(ahl)
Il tavolo marrone è davanti al letto.
of the

Il tavolo è _____ **letto.**

(frah)
**La lampada gialla è fra il tavolo
e il letto.**

La lampada gialla è _____ **il tavolo
e il letto.**

(ahl-leh)
Risponda alle domande, based on **le illustrazioni,** by filling in the blanks **con le**
to the

preposizioni corrette. Choose **le preposizioni** from those you have just learned.

Dov'è il libro rosso?

Il libro rosso è _____ **tavolo marrone.**

**Dov'è l'autobus
azzurro?**

L'autobus azzurro è _____ **all'albergo grigio.**

☐ **il giardino** *(jahr-dee-noh)* . . . . garden   _____
☐ **giugno** *(joon-yoh)* . . . . June   _____
☐ **il governo** *(goh-vehr-noh)* . . . . government   _____
☐ **grande** *(grahn-deh)* . . . . grand, big, large   _____
☐ **la guida** *(gwee-dah)* . . . . guide   _____

26

Dov'è la finestra? *(fee-neh-strah)* window **Dov'è il tappeto verde?** *(tahp-peh-toh)* carpet **Dov'è il vaso?** *(vah-soh)* vase

Il quadro è _____ alla finestra.

Il vaso è _____ tavolo nero.

Il quadro è _*sopra*_ il tavolo nero.

Il tappeto verde è _____ il tavolo nero.

Il tavolo nero è _____ il quadro.

Adesso, fill in each blank on **il palazzo** *(pah-lah-tsoh)* palace below **con** the best possible **preposizione.**

Le risposte corrette sono at the bottom of **la pagina. Buon divertimento.** have fun

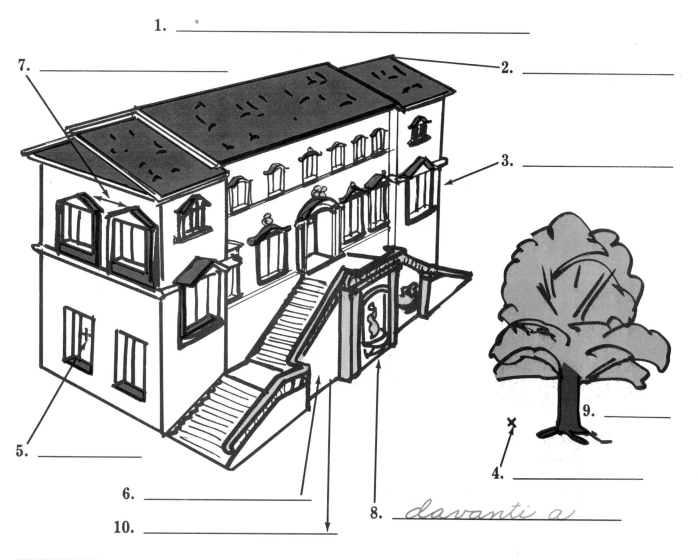

1. _____

7. _____   2. _____

3. _____

5. _____

6. _____

9. _____

4. _____

8. _*davanti a*_

10. _____

27

Step 9

(ah) (set-tem-breh) *(ah-pree-leh)(joon-yoh)* *(noh-vem-breh)*
Trenta giorni ha settembre, aprile, giugno e novembre . . .
has

(set-tee-mah-nah) *(moh-men-toh)*
Sound familiar? You have learned the days of **la settimana**, so **adesso è il momento**
it is the moment

(meh-see) *(ahn-noh)* *(tem-poh)*
to learn **i mesi dell'anno e** the different kinds of **tempo** you might encounter on your
months   of the   year   weather

(eh-sem-pee-oh) *(tem-poh)*
holiday. For **esempio,** you ask about **il tempo in italiano** just as you would **in inglese:**
example

(keh) *(fah)* *(doh-mahn-dah)* *(poh-ee)*
"Che tempo fa oggi?" Practice all the possible answers to this **domanda e poi**
does it make today   then

write **le risposte** in the blanks below.

(keh) (tem-poh) (fah) (oh-jee)
Che tempo fa oggi?
weather

(pee-oh-veh)
Piove oggi. _____
it rains

(neh-vee-kah)
Nevica oggi. _____
it snows

(fah) (freh-skoh)
Fa fresco oggi. _____
cool

(frehd-doh)
Fa freddo oggi. _____
cold

(tem-poh)
Fa bel tempo oggi. _____
nice

(kaht-tee-voh)
Fa cattivo tempo oggi. *Fa cattivo tempo oggi.*
bad

(kahl-doh)
Fa caldo oggi. _____
warm/hot

(cheh) (nehb-bee-ah)
C'è la nebbia oggi. _____
there is   fog

(poh-ee) *(noh-mee)*
Adesso, practice **le parole** on the next **pagina** aloud **e poi** fill in the blanks with **i nomi** of
then

(meh-see)
i mesi e the appropriate weather report. Notice that, **in italiano,** the months of the year
months

and the days of the week are not capitalized.

☐ **incantevole** *(een-kahn-teh-voh-leh)* . . . . enchanting, charming _____
☐ **indispensabile** *(een-dee-spen-sah-bee-leh)* . . . indispensable _____
☐ **l'individuo** *(leen-dee-vee-doo-oh)* . . . . individual (person) _____
☐ **l'industria** *(leen-doo-stree-ah)* . . . . industry _____
☐ **industrioso** *(een-doo-stree-oh-soh)* . . . . industrious _____

(een) (jehn-nah-ee-oh)
in gennaio _____   *(neh-vee-kah)*
Nevica in gennaio. _____

(fehb-brah-ee-oh)
in febbraio _____   **Nevica anche in febbraio.** _____
(ahn-keh)
also

(mar-tsoh)
in marzo *in marzo*   *(pee-oh-veh)*
Piove in marzo. _____

(ah-pree-leh)
in aprile _____   **Piove anche in aprile.** _____

(mah-joh)
in maggio _____   *(tee-rah) (vehn-toh)*
Tira vento in maggio. _____
it's   windy

(joon-yoh)
in giugno _____   *(cheh)(soh-leh)*
C'è sole in giugno. *C'è sole in giugno*
there is sun

(lool-yoh)
in luglio _____   **Fa bel tempo in luglio.** _____
(tem-poh)

(ah-goh-stoh)
in agosto _____   *(kahl-doh)*
Fa caldo in agosto. _____

(set-tem-breh)
in settembre _____   *(nehb-bee-ah)*
C'è la nebbia in settembre. _____
fog

(oht-toh-breh)
in ottobre _____   *(freh-skoh)*
Fa fresco in ottobre. _____

(noh-vem-breh)
in novembre _____   *(kaht-tee-voh)*
Fa cattivo tempo in novembre. _____

(dee-chem-breh)
in dicembre _____   *(frehd-doh)*
Fa freddo in dicembre. _____

Adesso, risponda alle domande based on **le illustrazioni** to the right.

Che tempo fa in febbraio? _____

Che tempo fa in aprile? _____

Che tempo fa in maggio? _____

Che tempo fa in agosto? *Fa* _____

Che tempo fa oggi, bello o cattivo? _____

□ **l'influenza** *(leen-floo-en-tsah)* . . . . influence _____
□ **l'informazione** *(leen-fohr-mah-tsee-oh-neh)* . . . information _____
□ **l'ingegnere** *(leen-jehn-yeh-reh)* . . . . engineer _____
□ **l'Inghilterra** *(leen-gheel-tehr-rah)* . . . . England _____
□ **innamorato** *(een-nah-moh-rah-toh)* . . . . enamored _____

Adesso, le stagioni dell'anno . . .
(stah-joh-nee) *(ahn-noh)*
seasons

(leen-vehr-noh) **l'inverno** winter	*(leh-stah-teh)* **l'estate** summer	*(lah-oo-toon-noh)* **l'autunno** autumn	*(pree-mah-veh-rah)* **la primavera** spring

_____	*l'estate*	_____	_____
Fa freddo	**Fa caldo**	*(tee-rah)* **Tira vento** it's	**Piove in**
(een) *(een-vehr-noh)* **in inverno.**	*(een)* *(eh-stah-teh)* **in estate.**	*(ah-oo-toon-noh)* **in autunno.**	*(pree-mah-veh-rah)* **primavera.**

At this point, **è una buona idea** to familiarize yourself **con le temperature europee.**
(eh) (oo-nah)(bwoh-nah) (ee-deh-ah) good idea *(tem-peh-rah-too-reh)* temperatures *(eh-oo-roh-peh)* European

Carefully read the typical weather forecasts below **e** study **il termometro,** because **le**
(tehr-moh-meh-troh) thermometer

temperature in Europa are calculated on the basis of Centigrade (not Fahrenheit).
(eh-oo-roh-pah)

Fahrenheit	Celsius	
212° F	——	100° C	*(ahk-kwah) (bohl-leh)* **l'acqua bolle** boils
98.6° F	——	37° C	**temperatura** *(sahn-goo-eh)* **normale del sangue** of blood
68° F	——	20° C	
32° F	——	0° C	*(dohl-cheh) (jeh-lah)* **l'acqua dolce gela** water fresh freezes
0° F	——	-17.8° C	*(sah-lah-tah)* **l'acqua salata gela** water salt freezes
-10° F	——	-23.3° C	

Il tempo per lunedì 21 marzo:

> **freddo con vento**
> *(tehm-peh-rah-too-rah)* *(grah-dee)*
> **temperatura: 5 gradi**
> degrees

Il tempo per martedì 18 luglio:

> **bello e caldo**
> nice
> **temperatura: 20 gradi**

☐ **l'insalata** *(leen-sah-lah-tah)* . . . . salad
☐ **interamente** *(een-teh-rah-men-teh)* . . . . entirely
☐ **interessante** *(een-teh-rehs-sahn-teh)* . . . . interesting
☐ **l'invito** *(leen-vee-toh)* . . . . invitation
☐ **l'isola** *(lee-soh-lah)* . . . . island

30

(fah-meel-yah) *(fah-meh)* *(feh-deh)*
Famiglia, fame, e fede
family   hunger   faith

Just as we have the three "R's" **in inglese, in italiano** there are the three "F's" which

help us to understand some of the basics of **la vita italiana.**
(vee-tah)(ee-tah-lee-ah-nah)
              life   Italian

 **F**amiglia    **F**ame   **F**ede

Study **le illustrazioni** below **e poi** write out **le nuove parole** in the blanks that follow.
(poh-ee)   *(noo-oh-vee)*
        then   new

(lah-beh-roh) *(jeh-neh-ah-loh-jee-koh)*
L'albero genealogico
tree   genealogical

(pah-oh-loh) *(bee-ahn-kee)*
Paolo Bianchi
(signor Bianchi)

(klah-oo-dee-ah)
Claudia Bianchi
(signora Bianchi)

(fee-leep-poh) *(mahn-freh-dee)*   *(sahn-drah)*
Filippo Manfredi   **Sandra Manfredi**
(signor Manfredi)   (signora Manfredi)

(nee-koh-lah)   *(mah-ree-ah)*
Nicola Bianchi   **Maria Bianchi**

(fah-meel-yah)
la famiglia
family

(joh-vahn-nee)   *(eh-leh-nah)*
Giovanni   **Elena**
(signor Bianchi)   (signorina Bianchi)

☐ **il lago** *(lah-goh)* . . . . lake   _____
☐ **largo** *(lahr-goh)* . . . . wide, broad   _____
☐ **il legume** *(leh-goo-meh)* . . . . vegetable   _____
☐ **la lettera** *(let-teh-rah)* . . . . letter   _____
☐ **la lezione** *(leh-tsee-oh-neh)* . . . . lesson, lecture   _____

i nonni *(ee)(nohn-nee)*
grandparents

il nonno *(nohn-noh)* _il nonno_
grandfather

la nonna *(nohn-nah)* _____
grandmother

i figli *(feel-yee)*
children

il figlio *(feel-yoh)* _____
son

la figlia *(feel-yah)* _____
daughter

i genitori *(jeh-nee-toh-ree)*
parents

il padre *(pah-dreh)* _____
father

la madre *(mah-dreh)* _____
mother

i parenti *(pah-ren-tee)*
relatives

lo zio *(zee-oh)* _____
uncle

la zia *(zee-ah)* _____
aunt

Il figlio e la figlia sono anche fratello *(frah-tel-loh)* **e sorella.** *(soh-rel-lah)*
also   brother   sister

Let's learn how to identify **la famiglia** *(fah-meel-yah)* by **nome.** *(noh-meh)* Study the following **esempi.** *(eh-sem-pee)*
examples

Come si chiama il padre? *(see) (kee-ah-mah)*
how   is   called   the father

Il padre si chiama _Nicola_ .

Come si chiama la madre? *(kee-ah-mah)*
is   called

La madre si chiama _Maria_ .
is   called

Adesso you fill in the following blanks, **basato** *(bah-sah-toh)* **sulle illustrazioni,** *(sool-leh)* in the same manner.
based   on the

Come si chiama _il figlio_ ?

_____ **si chiama** _____ .

Come si chiama _____ ?

_____ **si chiama** _____ .

☐ **libero** *(lee-beh-roh)* .... free, liberated
☐ **la lingua** *(leen-goo-ah)* .... language
☐ **la lista** *(lee-stah)* .... list
☐ **la lotteria** *(loht-teh-ree-ah)* .... lottery
☐ **lungo** *(loon-goh)* .... long

Study all these **illustrazioni e poi** practice

saying **e** writing out **le parole.**

Ecco la cucina.

(free-goh-ree-feh-roh)
il frigorifero

_____

(koo-chee-nah)
la cucina

_____

(vee-noh)
il vino

_____

(beer-rah)
la birra

_____

(laht-teh)
il latte

il latte

(boor-roh)
il burro

_____

Risponda alle domande aloud.

Dov'è la birra? . . . . *(free-goh-ree-feh-roh)*
La birra è nel frigorifero.

Dov'è il latte?   **Dov'è il vino?**   **Dov'è il burro?**

☐ **il maestro** *(mah-eh-stroh)* . . . . master, teacher
☐ **magnifico** *(mahn-yee-fee-koh)* . . . . magnificent
☐ **la maniera** *(mah-nee-eh-rah)* . . . . manner, way
☐ **marzo** *(mahr-tsoh)* . . . . March
☐ **il matrimonio** *(mah-tree-moh-nee-oh)* . . . marriage

_____
_____
_____
_____
_____

33

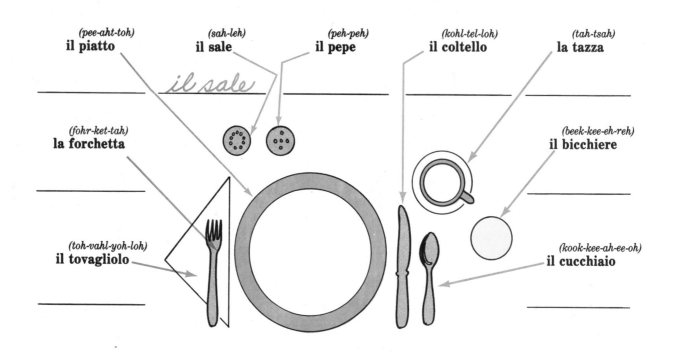

(pee-aht-toh)
il piatto

(sah-leh)
il sale

(peh-peh)
il pepe

(kohl-tel-loh)
il coltello

(tah-tsah)
la tazza

il sale

(fohr-ket-tah)
la forchetta

(beek-kee-eh-reh)
il bicchiere

(toh-vahl-yoh-loh)
il tovagliolo

(kook-kee-ah-ee-oh)
il cucchiaio

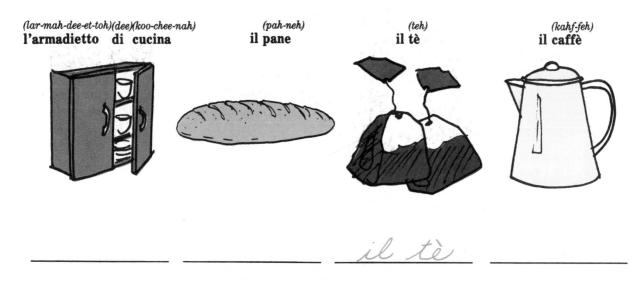

(lar-mah-dee-et-toh)(dee)(koo-chee-nah)
l'armadietto di cucina

(pah-neh)
il pane

(teh)
il tè

(kahf-feh)
il caffè

_____   _____   *il tè*   _____

Dov'è il pane? Il pane è nell'armadietto. Dov'è il tè? Dov'è il caffè? Dov'è il sale? Dov'è il pepe? Adesso apra *(ah-prah)* (open) your **libro** to the **pagina con** the labels **e** remove the next **diciannove** *(dee-chahn-noh-veh)* labels **e** proceed to label all these **cose** in your **casa.** Do not forget to use every opportunity to say these **parole** out loud. **È molto importante!** *(eem-por-tahn-teh)*

☐ **il medico** *(meh-dee-koh)* .... medical doctor, physician
☐ **la memoria** *(meh-moh-ree-ah)* .... memory
☐ **meno** *(meh-noh)* .... minus, less
☐ **meraviglioso** *(meh-rah-veel-yoh-soh)* .... marvelous
34 ☐ **il mercato** *(mehr-kah-toh)* .... market

_____
_____
_____
_____

In Italia, there is not the wide variety of **religioni** *(reh-lee-joh-nee)* that **abbiamo** *(ahb-bee-ah-moh)(kwee)* **qui** in America.
religions   we have   here

A person's **religione è generalmente** *(reh-lee-joh-neh)* *(jeh-neh-rahl-men-teh)* one of the following.
generally

1. ***cattolica** *(kaht-toh-lee-kah)* _cattolica_
Catholic

2. **protestante** *(proh-teh-stahn-teh)* _____
Protestant

3. **ebraica,   ebreo** *(eh-brah-ee-kah) (eh-breh-oh)* _____
Jewish

Ecco una cattedrale *(kaht-teh-drah-leh)* in **Italia.**
cathedral

È una cattedrale cattolica o

protestante?

È una nuova cattedrale? No, è una

vecchia cattedrale. *(vehk-kee-ah)* You will see
old
molte belle cattedrali *(mohl-teh) (bel-leh) (kaht-teh-drah-lee)* like this
many   beautiful

during your holiday **in Italia.**

Adesso let's learn how to say "I am" **in italiano:** I am = **io   sono** *(ee-oh) (soh-noh)* _____.

Practice saying **"io sono" con** the following **parole. Adesso** write each sentence for more

practice.

Io sono cattolico. _____   **Io sono protestante.** _____

Io sono ebreo. _Io sono ebreo._   **Io sono americano.** _____

Io sono in Europa. *(eh-oo-roh-pah)* _____   **Io sono in Italia.** _____

*To make an adjective feminine **in italiano,** you usually change the **o** at the end of the word to an **a.**
Adjectives that end in **e** are both masculine and feminine.

- ☐ **il metallo** *(meh-tahl-loh)* .... metal _____
- ☐ **il metro** *(meh-troh)* .... meter _____
- ☐ **milione** *(mee-lee-oh-neh)* .... million _____
- ☐ **la misura** *(mee-soo-rah)* .... measure, size _____
- ☐ **la moda** *(moh-dah)* .... style, fashion, mode _____

Io sono nella *(nel-lah)* *(kee-eh-sah)* chiesa. _____   Io sono nella cucina. *(koo-chee-nah)* _____
in the church   kitchen

Io sono la madre. *Io sono la madre.*   Io sono il padre. _____

Io sono nell'albergo. _____   Io sono stanco. *(stahn-koh)* _____
tired

Adesso identify all **le** *(pehr-soh-neh)* **persone nell'illustrazione** below. On the **linee,** *(lee-neh)* write **le parole**
people   lines

corrette in italiano for each **persona** corresponding to **il numero** **sotto** *(soht-toh)* **l'illustrazione**
under

(een-dee-vee-doo-ah-leh) **individuale.**
individual

1. _____   2. _____

3. _____   4. _____

5.   *la zia*   6. _____

7. _____

Don't be afraid of all the extra apostrophes and accents **in italiano.** Just concentrate on

your easy pronunciation guide and remember: practice, practice, practice.

☐ **il motore** *(moh-toh-reh)* .... motor, engine
☐ **il momento** *(moh-men-toh)* .... moment
  —**Un momento!** .... Just a moment!
☐ **la montagna** *(mohn-tahn-yah)* .... mountain
☐ **il museo** *(moo-seh-oh)* .... museum

_____
_____
_____
_____
_____

(eem-pah-rah-reh)
Imparare!
to learn

(leh-ee) *(ah-veh-reh)* *(voh-reh-ee)* *(koh-stah-reh)* *(ahr-ree-vah-reh)* *(ehn-trah-reh)* *(veh-nee-reh)*
Lei have already used the verbs **avere** and **vorrei,** **costare,** **arrivare,** **entrare,** **venire,**
you   to have   would like   to cost   to arrive   to enter   to come

(ree-spohn-deh-reh) *(ree-peh-teh-reh)* *(eh)* *(soh-noh)*
rispondere, ripetere, è and **sono.** Although you might be able to "get by" **con** these
to respond   to repeat   is   are

(vehr-bee) *(mehl-yoh)*
verbi, let's assume you want to do **meglio** than that. First, a quick review.
better

How do you say ⬜ **"I"** in italiano? *io*   How do you say ⬜ **"we"** in italiano? _____

Compare these **due** charts

(eem-pah-ree)
very carefully **e impari** these
learn

sette parole on the right.

I =	*(ee-oh)* **io**		we =	*(noh-ee)* **noi**	
he =	*(loo-ee)* **lui**		you =	*(leh-ee)* **Lei**	
she =	*(leh-ee)* **lei**		they =	*(loh-roh)* **loro**	

(lee-neh) *(frah)* *(een-gleh-see)* *(ee-tah-lee-ah-neh)* *(leh-ee)*
Adesso draw **linee fra** the matching **parole inglesi e parole italiane** below to see if **Lei**
between   you

can keep these **parole** straight in your mind.

Note: **Lei,** with a capital "l" means you; **lei,** with a lower case "l," means she.

lei	he
loro	she
noi	I
Lei	they
io	we
lui	you

(fohl-yoh)
Adesso close **il libro e** write out both columns of the above practice on **un foglio di**
piece

(kahr-tah) *(leh-ee)* *(beh-neh)* *(mah-leh)* *(nohn)*
carta. How did **Lei** do? **Bene o male? Non bene o non male? Adesso** that **Lei** know
paper   good   bad   not   good   not   bad

(keh) *(deh-see-deh-rah)*
these **parole,** you will soon be able to say almost anything **che Lei desidera** by using
that   desire

a type of "plug-in" formula.

☐ **la musica** *(moo-see-kah)* .... music   _____
☐ **nativo** *(nah-tee-voh)* .... native   _____
☐ **naturale** *(nah-too-rah-leh)* .... natural   _____
☐ **la nazione** *(nah-tsee-oh-neh)* .... nation, country   _____
☐ **necessario** *(neh-chehs-sah-ree-oh)* .... necessary   _____

To demonstrate, here are **sei esempi** *(seh-ee)* of some very practical **e** important **verbi italiani.**

These are **verbi** whose basic form ends in **"are."** Write **i verbi** in the blanks below after **Lei** have practiced them out loud many times.

(pahr-lah-reh)
parlare = to speak

(reh-stah-reh)
restare = to remain/stay

(ah-bee-tah-reh)
abitare = to live/reside

_____

restare

_____

(ohr-dee-nah-reh)
ordinare = to order

(kohm-prah-reh)
comprare = to buy

(kee-ah-mahr-see)
chiamarsi = to be called

_____

_____

_____

Study the following verb patterns **con attenzione.**
(aht-tehn-tsee-oh-neh)
attention

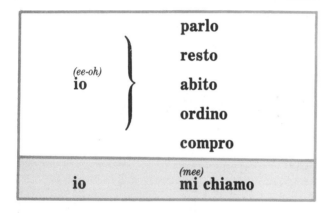

io *(ee-oh)* }	parlo resto abito ordino compro
io	**mi chiamo** *(mee)*

lui *(loo-ee)* lei *(leh-ee)* Lei *(leh-ee)* }	parla resta abita ordina compra
lui lei Lei }	**si chiama** *(see)*

Note: • With **io**, you drop the final **"are"** from the basic verb form and add an **"o."**

• With **lui, lei** and **Lei**, you simply drop the final **"are"** and add **"a."**

(kee-ah-mahr-see)
• **Chiamarsi** varies but not too much. It is a very important verb, so take a few extra minutes to learn it.

•Some **verbi italiani** will not conform to the rules quite as easily as these **verbi** do. But don't worry . . . you will be perfectly understood whether you say **"parlo"** or **"parla."**

(l-yee)
Gli Italiani will be delighted that you have taken the time to learn their language.
the

☐ **il nome** *(noh-meh)* . . . . name _____

☐ **nord** *(nord)* . . . . north _____

☐ **normale** *(nor-mahl-leh)* . . . . normal _____

☐ **la notizia** *(noh-tee-tsee-ah)* . . . . news, notice _____

☐ **nuovo** *(noo-oh-voh)* . . . . new _____

38

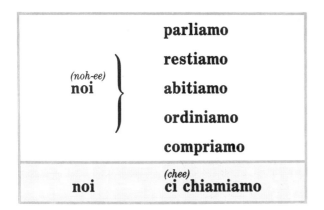

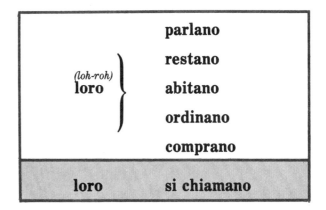

Here are a few hints for mixing and matching **verbi** and their subjects.

-iamo ⟶ noi   ex.   **noi parliamo**

-o ⟶ io   ex.   **io parlo**

-ano ⟶ loro   ex.   **loro parlano**

Adesso, read through the entire verb form aloud several times before writing out each

form in the blank below.

(pahr-lah-reh) **parlare** to speak	*(reh-stah-reh)* **restare** to remain/stay
Io *parlo/* _____ italiano.	**Io** *resto/* _____ in Italia.
Lui Lei (she) *parla/* _____ italiano.	**Lui Lei** (she) *resta/* _____ in America.
Noi *parliamo/* _____ italiano.	**Noi** *restiamo/* _____ in Europa.
Lei (you) *parla/* _____ inglese.	**Lei** (you) *resta/* _____ nell'albergo.
Loro *parlano/* _____ inglese.	**Loro** *restano/* _____ in Francia.

☐ **l'occasione** *(lohk-kah-see-oh-neh)* . . . . occasion, opportunity
☐ **occupato** *(ohk-koo-pah-toh)* . . . . occupied, busy
☐ **l'odore** *(loh-doh-reh)* . . . . odor
☐ **l'oggetto** *(loh-jet-toh)* . . . . object
☐ **l'ombrello** *(lohm-brel-loh)* . . . . umbrella

39

(ah-bee-tah-reh)
abitare
to live/reside

Io _abito/_____ in Italia.

Lui _____ in America.
Lei (she)

Noi _____ in **(een-gheel-tehr-rah)**
Inghilterra.
England

Lei (you) _____ in Europa.

Loro _____ in **(chee-nah)**
Cina.
China

(kohm-prah-reh)
comprare
to buy

Io _compro/_____ un libro.

Lui _____ un'insalata.
Lei

Noi _____ una macchina.

Lei _____ un orologio.

Loro _____ una lampada.

(kee-ah-mahr-see)
chiamarsi
to be called

Io _mi chiamo/_____ Maria Sandini.

Lui _si chiama/_____ Mauro.
Lei

Noi _ci chiamiamo/_____ Smith.

Lei _si chiama/_____ Martini.

Loro _si chiamano/_____ Verdi.

(or-dee-nah-reh)
ordinare
to order

Io _ordino/_____ un **(beek-kee-eh-reh)**
bicchiere di acqua.

Lui _____ un bicchiere di vino.
Lei

Noi _____ una tazza di tè.

Lei _____ una tazza di caffè.

Loro _____ bicchiere di **(laht-teh)**
latte.
milk

Remember these **verbi**?

(veh-nee-reh)
venire = to come

venire
_____

(ahn-dah-reh)
andare = to go

_____

(eem-pah-rah-reh)
imparare = to learn

_____

(voh-reh-ee)
vorrei = would like

_____

(ah-veh-reh)
avere = to have

_____

(ah-veh-reh)(bee-sohn-yoh) (dee)
avere bisogno di = to need
to have   need   of

_____

Here we have **sei,** **(seh-ee)** already familiar **verbi** whose following forms might seem a bit erratic

after our last group. DON'T PANIC or give up. Read them out loud, practice them, think

of their **similitudini,** **(see-mee-lee-too-dee-nee)** write them out and **poi** **(poh-ee)** try to use them in sentences of your own.
similarities   then

☐ **l'opera** (loh-peh-rah) .... opera   _____
☐ **l'ora** (loh-rah) .... hour, time   _____
☐ **ordinario** (ohr-dee-nah-ree-oh) .... ordinary   _____
☐ **l'ospedale** (loh-speh-dah-leh) .... hospital   _____
40 ☐ **ovest** (oh-vest) .... west   _____

Think of how hard it would be to speak **in inglese** with no verbs—it's the same **in italiano**.

(veh-nee-reh)
venire
to come

Io *vengo* dall'America.

Lui *viene* dall'Inghilterra.
Lei (she)

Noi *veniamo* dal Canada. *(kah-nah-dah)*

Lei (you) *viene* da Nuova York.

Loro *vengono* da Roma. *(roh-mah)*
Rome

(ahn-dah-reh)
andare
to go

Io *vado* in Italia.

Lui *va* in Francia. *(frahn-chah)*
Lei (she) France

Noi *andiamo* in Spagna. *(spahn-yah)*
Spain

Lei (you) *va* in Europa.

Loro *vanno* in Cina.

(eem-pah-rah-reh)
imparare
to learn

Io *imparo* l'italiano.

Lui _____ l'inglese.
Lei

Noi _____ la geometria. *(jeh-oh-meh-tree-ah)*
geometry

Lei _____ il tedesco. *(teh-deh-skoh)*
German

Loro _____ il francese. *(frahn-cheh-seh)*

(voh-reh-ee)
vorrei
would like

Io *vorrei* un bicchiere di vino.

Lui *vorrebbe* un bicchiere di vino rosso.
Lei

Noi *vorremmo* un bicchiere di vino bianco.

Lei *vorrebbe* un bicchiere di latte.

Loro *vorrebbero* un bicchiere di birra.

(ah-veh-reh)
avere
to have

Io *ho* mille lire.

Lui *ha* due mila lira.
Lei

Noi *abbiamo* cento lire.

Lei *ha* cinquecento lire.

Loro *hanno* cento mila lire.

(ah-veh-reh) *(bee-sohn-yoh)* *(dee)*
avere bisogno di
to have   need   of

Io *ho bisogno di* una camera. *(kah-meh-rah)*
room

Lui *ha bisogno di* una camera.
Lei

Noi *abbiamo bisogno di* una camera.

Lei *ha bisogno di* una camera.

Loro *hanno bisogno di* una camera.

☐ **il pacco** *(pahk-koh)* . . . . package
☐ **il paio** *(pah-ee-oh)* . . . . pair
  — **un paio di scarpe** . . . . a pair of shoes
☐ **il palazzo** *(pah-lah-tsoh)* . . . . palace, building
☐ **i pantaloni** *(pahn-tah-loh-nee)* . . . . pants, trousers

41

Adesso take a deep breath. See if **Lei** (leh-ee) can fill in the blanks below. **Le risposte corrette sono** at the bottom of **la pagina.**

1. I speak Italian. _____

2. He comes from America. _____

3. We learn Italian. _____

4. They have 1000 lire. _____

5. She would like a glass of water. _____

6. We need a room. *Abbiamo bisogno di una camera.*

7. My name is Paul Smith. _____

8. I live in America. _____

9. You are buying a book. _____

10. He orders a beer. _____

In the following Steps, **Lei** will be introduced to more **e** more **verbi e** should drill them in exactly the same way as **Lei** did in this section. Look up **le parole nuove** (noo-oh-veh) in your **dizionario** (dee-tsee-oh-nah-ree-oh) **e** make up your own sentences using the same type of pattern. Try out your
dictionary

parole nuove for that's how you make them yours to use on your holiday. Remember, the more **Lei** practice **adesso,** the more enjoyable your trip will be. **Buona fortuna!**

Adesso is a perfect time to turn to the back of **il libro,** clip out your flash cards **e** start flashing.

Be sure to check off your free **parole** in the box provided as **Lei impara** (eem-pah-rah) each one.
learn

(leh) *(oh-reh)*
Le Ore
hours

Lei know how to tell **i giorni** *(johr-nee)* **della settimana e i mesi dell'anno,** so **adesso** let's learn
days   week   months   year

to tell time. As a **viaggiatore** *(vee-ah-jah-toh-reh)* **in Italia, Lei** need to be able to tell time for
traveler

(preh-noh-tah-tsee-oh-nee)
prenotazioni, appuntamenti e treni. Ecco the "basics."
reservations

What time is it? = **Che ora è?** *(oh-rah)*	
_____	

half past	=	**e mezzo** *(meh-zoh)* _____
less	=	**meno** *(meh-noh)* *meno*
midnight	=	**mezzanotte** *(meh-zah-noht-teh)* _____
noon	=	**mezzogiorno** *(meh-zoh-johr-noh)* _____

Sono le cinque. *(cheen-kweh)*
it is   five o'clock

È mezzogiorno. *(meh-zoh-johr-noh)*

Sono le sette e quaranta.

Sono le quattro e mezzo.

O

Sono le tre.

Sono le otto e venti.

Sono le otto meno venti.
eight   minus   twenty

Sono le due e mezzo.

Adesso fill in the blanks according to **l'ora** indicated **sull'orologio.**
on the

Sono le _____.

Sono le _____.

Sono le _____.

Sono le _____.

È l' _____.

Sono le *quattro*.

Sono le _____.

Sono le _____.

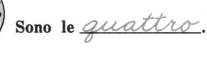

Ecco more time-telling *(pah-roh-leh)* **parole** to add to your *(pah-roh-lah)* **parola** power.

(kwahr-toh) **un quarto**	= a quarter
(meh-noh) **meno un quarto**	= a quarter to
e un quarto	= a quarter past

Sono le due e un quarto. O **Sono le due e quindici.**
it is

Sono le due meno un quarto. O **È l'una e quarantacinque.**

Adesso, your turn.

Sono le *tre e un quarto* .

 Sono le _____ .

 Sono le _____ .

 Sono le _____ .

I numeri — see how **importanti** they have become! **Adesso, risponda alle domande**
(seh-gwen-tee)
seguenti based on **gli orologi** below.
following

| **Che ora è?** |

1. _____

2. *Sono le sette e mezzo.*

3. _____

4. _____

5. _____

6. _____

7. _____

44

When **Lei** answer a "**quando**" *(kwahn-doh)* question, say "**alle**" *(ah-leh)* before you give the time.

when · *at*

TRENO 43 | **6:00**

Quando arriva il treno? _____alle sei_____ .

Adesso, risponda alle domande seguenti *(seh-gwen-tee)* based on **gli orologi** *(l-yee)* below. Be sure to practice

following

saying each question out loud several times.

(kwahn-doh) *(koh-meen-chah)* *(kohn-chehr-toh)*
Quando comincia il concerto? _____ .

begins · *concert*

Quando comincia il film? *(feelm)* _____ .

Quando arriva l'autobus giallo? _____ .

Quando arriva il tassì? _____ .

(ah-pehr-toh)
Quando è aperto il ristorante? _____alle cinque_____ .

open

(kee-oo-soh)
Quando è chiuso il ristorante? _____ .

closed

(ah-leh) *(dee)* *(see)* *(dee-cheh)*
Alle otto di mattina, si dice,

at · *in the* · *one* · *says*

(seen-yoh-rah)
"Buon giorno, signora Fellini."

Mrs.

All'una del pomeriggio, si dice,

(seen-yohr)
"Buon giorno, signor Franchi."

Mr.

Alle otto di sera, si dice,

(seen-yoh-ree-nah)
"Buona sera, signorina Bianchi."

Miss

Alle dieci di sera, si dice,

"Buona notte."

☐ **il Papa** *(pah-pah)* .... Pope _____
☐ **il parcheggio** *(pahr-keh-joh)* .... parking place, parking lot _____
☐ **il parco** *(pahr-koh)* .... park _____
☐ **Parigi** *(pah-ree-jee)* .... Paris _____
☐ **la parte** *(pahr-teh)* .... part, portion _____

45

Remember:

| What time is it? = **Che ora è?** | When/at what time = **Quando?** **A che ora?** |

Can **Lei** pronounce **e** understand **il**

(pah-rah-grah-foh) *(seh-gwen-teh)*
paragrafo seguente?
paragraph

> **Il treno di Parigi arriva alle 15,15.**
>
> **Sono adesso le 15,20. Il treno**
>
> *(ree-tahr-doh)*
> **è in ritardo. Il treno arriva oggi**
> late
>
> **alle 17,15. Domani il treno arriva**
>
> *(dee) (noo-oh-voh)*
> **di nuovo alle 15,15.**
> again

Ecco more practice exercises. **Risponda alle domande** based on **l'ora** given.

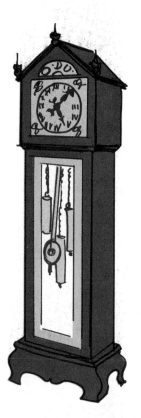

Che ora è?

1. (1:30) _____

2. (6:30) _____

3. (2:15) *Sono le due e un quarto.*

4. (11:40) _____

5. (12:18) _____

6. (7:20) _____

7. (3:10) _____

8. (4:05) _____

9. (5:35) _____

10. (11:50) _____

Note: When writing the time, Italians use a comma instead of a colon to separate the hour from the minutes (*e.g.,* 7,30).

☐ **la partenza** *(pahr-ten-tsah)* . . . . departure _____
☐ **il passaporto** *(pahs-sah-pohr-toh)* . . . . . . passport _____
☐ **la pasta** *(pah-stah)* . . . . pasta (**fettucine, ravioli,** etc.) _____
☐ **la patata** *(pah-tah-tah)* . . . . potato _____
46 ☐ **la penna** *(pen-nah)* . . . . pen _____

Ecco a quick quiz. Fill in the blanks **con i numeri corretti. Le risposte sono sotto.**
(soht-toh)
below

1. **Un minuto ha** *(mee-noo-toh) (ah)* _____ **secondi.** *(seh-kohn-dee)*
   has (?)

5. **Un mese ha** _trenta_ **giorni.**
   (?)

2. **Un'ora ha** _____ **minuti.** *(mee-noo-tee)*
   (?)

6. **Un anno ha** _____ **mesi.**
   (?)

3. **Un giorno ha** _____ **ore.**
   (?)

7. **Un anno ha** _____ **settimane.**
   (?)

4. **Una settimana ha** _____ **giorni.** *(johr-nee)*
   (?)

8. **Un anno ha** _____ **giorni.**
   (?)

Ecco a sample **pagina** from **un orario di FFSS** *(oh-rah-ree-oh) (eh-feh)(eh-feh)(eh-seh)(eh-seh)* — the Italian national railroad.
timetable

Un rapido (RAP) *(rah-pee-doh)* **e un espresso (ESP)** *(es-pres-soh)* **sono molto rapidi.** *(rah-pee-dee)* **Un diretto (DIR)** *(dee-ret-toh)* **e un**
fast

direttissimo (DIR.MO) sono rapidi. Un accelerato (ACC) *(ah-cheh-leh-rah-toh)* **è molto lento** *(len-toh)* and stops at every
slow

small station along the way.

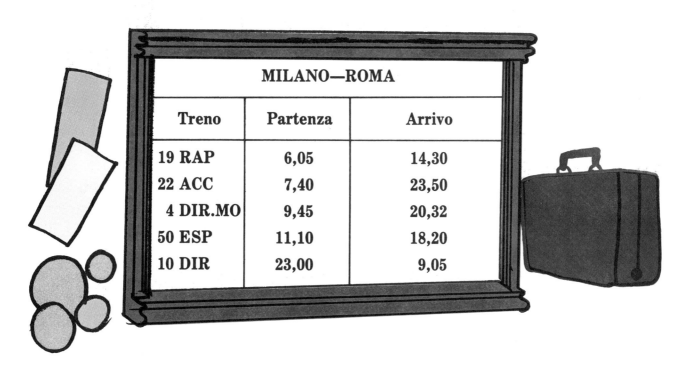

MILANO—ROMA		
Treno	Partenza	Arrivo
19 RAP	6,05	14,30
22 ACC	7,40	23,50
4 DIR.MO	9,45	20,32
50 ESP	11,10	18,20
10 DIR	23,00	9,05

RISPOSTE

1. sessanta 2. sessanta 3. ventiquattro 4. sette 5. trenta 6. dodici 7. cinquantadue 8. trecento sessantacinque

47

Ecco tre verbi nuovi ^(pehr) per Step 12.
for

^(dee-reh)
dire = to say

^(mahn-jah-reh)
mangiare = to eat

^(beh-reh)
bere = to drink

dire _____ _____

^(dee-reh)
dire
to say

Io _dico/_ _____ "Buon giorno."

Lui _dice/_ _____ "Ciao."
Lei (she)

Noi _diciamo/_ _____ "No."

Lei (you) _dice/_ _____ "Sì."

Loro non _dicono/_ _____ ^(nee-ehn-teh) **niente.**
nothing

^(mahn-jah-reh)
mangiare
to eat

Io _mangio/_ _____ la **minestra.** ^(mee-neh-strah)
soup

Lui _____ la **bistecca.** ^(bee-stehk-kah)
Lei beefsteak

Noi _____ **molto.**

Lei non _____ **niente.** ^(nee-en-teh)
nothing

Loro _____ i **ravioli.** ^(rah-vee-oh-lee)

^(beh-reh)
bere
to drink

Io _bevo/_ _____ il **latte.**

Lui _beve/_ _____ il **vino bianco.**
Lei

Noi _beviamo/_ _____ la **birra.**

Lei _beve/_ ____ un **bicchiere di acqua.**

Loro _bevono/_ _____ il **tè.**

Have you noticed that, to make a plural **in italiano,** you don't add an **"s"** to the end of the

word? Instead, the final **"o"** or **"e"** changes to **"i,"** and the final **"a"** changes to **"e."**

☐ **perfetto** _(pehr-fet-toh)_ . . . . perfect _____
☐ **il periodo** _(peh-ree-oh-doh)_ . . . . period _____
☐ **la permanenza** _(pehr-mah-nen-tsah)_ . . . . . stay, permanence _____
☐ **il permesso** _(pehr-mehs-soh)_ . . . . permission _____
— **Permesso?** . . . . May I pass through? _____

(kwah-droh)
il **quadro**

(sohf-fee-toh)
il **soffitto**

(lahn-goh-loh)
l'**angolo**

(fee-neh-strah)
la **finestra**

(soh-fah)
il **sofà**

(seh-dee-ah)
la **sedia**

(tahp-peh-toh)
il **tappeto**

(tah-voh-loh)
il **tavolo**

(pohr-tah)
la **porta**

(loh-roh-loh-joh)
l'**orologio**

(ten-dee-nah)
la **tendina**

(pah-reh-teh)
la **parete**

(kah-sah)
la **casa**

(sah-lah) (dah) (prahn-zoh)
la **sala da pranzo**

(sah-loht-toh)
il **salotto**

(kah-meh-rah) (dah) (let-toh)
la **camera da letto**

(stahn-zah) (dah) (bahn-yoh)
la **stanza da bagno**

(koo-chee-nah)
la **cucina**

(loof-fee-choh)
l'**ufficio**

(kahn-tee-nah)
la **cantina**

(gah-rahzh)
il **garage**

(lah-oo-toh)
l'**auto**

(mahk-kee-nah)
la **macchina**

(bee-chee-klet-tah)
la **bicicletta**

(kah-neh)
il **cane**

(gaht-toh)
il **gatto**

(jahr-dee-noh)
il **giardino**

(poh-stah)
la **posta**

(boo-kah) (del-leh) (let-teh-reh)
la **buca delle lettere**

(fee-oh-ree)
i **fiori**

(kahm-pah-nel-loh)
il **campanello**

(oo-noh)
1 **uno**

(doo-eh)
2 **due**

(treh)
3 **tre**

(kwaht-troh)
4 **quattro**

(cheen-kweh)
5 **cinque**

(seh-ee)
6 **sei**

(set-teh)
7 **sette**

(oht-toh)
8 **otto**

(noh-veh)
9 **nove**

(dee-eh-chee)
10 **dieci**

(bee-ahn-koh)
bianco

(neh-roh)
nero

(jahl-loh)
giallo

(rohs-soh)
rosso

(ah-zoor-roh)
azzurro

(gree-joh)
grigio

(mahr-roh-neh)
marrone

(vehr-deh)
verde

(roh-sah)
rosa

(mool-tee-koh-loh-reh)
multicolore

(loo-neh-dee)
lunedì

(mahr-teh-dee)
martedì

(mehr-koh-leh-dee)
mercoledì

(joh-veh-dee)
giovedì

(veh-nehr-dee)
venerdì

(sah-bah-toh)
sabato

(doh-meh-nee-kah)
domenica

(bwohn) (johr-noh)
buon giorno

(bwoh-nah) (seh-rah)
buona sera

(bwoh-nah) (noht-teh)
buona notte

(chah-oh)
ciao

(lahm-pah-dah)
il la **lampada**

(loo-cheh)
la **luce**

(vee-noh)
il **vino**

(beer-rah)
la **birra**

(laht-teh)
il **latte**

(boor-roh)
il **burro**

(pee-aht-toh)
il **piatto**

(sah-leh)
il **sale**

(peh-peh)
il **pepe**

(kohl-tel-loh)
il **coltello**

(tah-tsah)
la **tazza**

(fohr-ket-tah)
la **forchetta**

(bee-kee-eh-reh)
il **bicchiere**

(toh-vahl-yoh-loh)
il **tovagliolo**

(kook-kee-ah-ee-oh)
il **cucchiaio**

(lar-mah-dee-et-toh) (koo-chee-nah)
l'**armadietto di cucina**

STICKY LABELS

This book has over 150 special sticky labels for you to use as you learn new words. When you are introduced to a word, remove the corresponding label from these pages. Be sure to use each of these unique labels by adhering them to a picture, window, lamp, or whatever object it refers to. The sticky labels make learning to speak Italian much more fun and a lot easier than you ever expected.

For example, when you look in the mirror and see the label, say

(loh)   *(spek-kee-oh)*
"lo specchio."

Don't just say it once, say it again and again.

And once you label the refrigerator, you should never again open that door without saying

(eel)   *(free-goh-ree-feh-roh)*
" il frigorifero."

By using the sticky labels, you not only learn new words but friends and family learn along with you!

(pah-neh)
il **pane**

(teh)
il **tè**

(kahf-feh)
il **caffè**

(choh-koh-lah-toh)
il **cioccolato**

(lah-kwah)
l'**acqua**

(let-toh)
il **letto**

(koh-pehr-tah)
la **coperta**

(koo-shee-noh)
il **cuscino**

(zvel-yah)
la **sveglia**

(lahr-mah-dee-oh)
l'**armadio**

(lah-vahn-dee-noh)
il **lavandino**

(doh-chah)
la **doccia**

(vee-chee)
il **W.C.**

(spehk-kee-oh)
lo **specchio**

(gwahn-toh) (dah) (bahn-yoh)
il **guanto da bagno**

(lah-shoo-gah-mah-noh)
l'**asciugamano**

(lah-shoo-gah-mah-noh) (peek-koh-loh)
l'**asciugamano piccolo**

(lah-shoo-gah-mah-noh) (bahn-yoh)
l'**asciugamano da bagno**

(mah-tee-tah)
la **matita**

(pen-nah)
la **penna**

(kahr-tah)
la **carta**

(let-teh-rah)
la **lettera**

(kahr-toh-lee-nah)
la **cartolina**

(frahn-koh-bohl-loh)
il **francobollo**

(lee-broh)
il **libro**

(ree-vee-stah)
la **rivista**

(johr-nah-leh)
il **giornale**

(ohk-kee-ah-lee)
gli **occhiali**

(teh-leh-vee-soh-reh)
il **televisore**

(cheh-stee-noh)
il **cestino**

(pahs-sah-pohr-toh)
il **passaporto**

(beel-yet-toh)
il **biglietto**

(vah-lee-jah)
la **valigia**

(bohr-sah)
la **borsa**

(pohr-tah-fohl-yoh)
il **portafoglio**

(deh-nah-roh)
il **denaro**

(mahk-kee-nah) (foh-toh-grah-fee-kah)
la **macchina fotografica**

(pel-lee-koh-lah)
la **pellicola**

(koh-stoo-meh) (dah) (bahn-yoh)
il **costume da bagno**

(sahn-dah-lee)
i **sandali**

(sah-poh-neh)
il **sapone**

(spah-tsoh-lee-noh) (dah) (den-tee)
lo **spazzolino da denti**

(den-tee-free-choh)
il **dentifricio**

(pet-tee-neh)
il **pettine**

(soh-prah-bee-toh)
il **soprabito**

(leem-pehr-meh-ah-bee-leh)
l'**impermeabile**

(lohm-brel-loh)
l'**ombrello**

(gwahn-tee)
i **guanti**

(kahp-pel-loh)
il **cappello**

(stee-vah-lee)
gli **stivali**

(skahr-peh)
le **scarpe**

(kahl-tsee-nee)
i **calzini**

(kahl-tseh)
le **calze**

(pee-jah-mah)
il **pigiama**

(kah-mee-cheh-tah)(dah) (noht-teh)
la **camicetta da notte**

(lahk-kahp-pah-toh-ee-oh)
l'**accappatoio**

(pahn-toh-foh-leh)
le **pantofole**

(soh-noh) (ah-meh-ree-kah-noh)
Sono americano.

(vohr-reh-ee) (eem-pah-rah-reh) (lee-tah-lee-ah-noh)
Vorrei imparare l'italiano.

(mee) (kee-ah-moh)
Mi chiamo _____.

(lah-bee-toh)
l'**abito**

(krah-vaht-tah)
la **cravatta**

(fah-tsoh-let-toh)
il **fazzoletto**

(kah-mee-chah)
la **camicia**

(jahk-kah)
la **giacca**

(pahn-tah-loh-nee)
i **pantaloni**

(veh-stee-toh)
il **vestito**

(kah-mee-chet-tah)
la **camicetta**

(gohn-nah)
la **gonna**

(mahl-yah)
la **maglia**

(reh-jee-pet-toh)
il **reggipetto**

(soht-toh-veh-steh)
la **sottoveste**

(kah-noht-tee-eh-rah)
la **canottiera**

(moo-tahn-deh)
le **mutande**

(bwohn) (ahp-peh-tee-toh)
buon appetito

(ohk-koo-pah-toh)
occupato

(mee) (skoo-see)
mi scusi

PLUS . . .

Your book includes a number of other innovative features. At the back of the book, you'll find seven pages of flash cards. Cut them out and flip through them at least once a day.

On pages 112 and 113, you'll find a beverage guide and a menu guide. Don't wait until your trip to use them. Clip out the menu guide and use it tonight at the dinner table. And use the beverage guide to practice ordering your favorite drinks.

By using the special features in this book, you will be speaking Italian before you know it.

(bwohn) *(dee-vehr-tee-men-toh)*
Buon divertimento!
have fun

Nord - Sud, Est - Ovest
(nord) north (sood) south (est) east (oh-vest) west

If **Lei** are looking at **una carta** *(kahr-tah)* **geografica** *(jeh-oh-grah-fee-kah)* **e Lei** see **le parole seguenti,** it should
map

not be too **difficile** *(dee-fee-chee-leh)* to figure out what they mean. Take an educated guess. **Le**
difficult

risposte sono sotto.

l'America del nord *(lah-meh-ree-kah) (del) (nord)*	**l'America del sud** *(lah-meh-ree-kah) (sood)*	**la Germania dell'ovest** *(jehr-mah-nee-ah) (oh-vest)*
il Mare del nord *(mah-reh)*	**l'Africa del sud** *(lah-free-kah)*	**la Germania dell'est** *(jehr-mah-nee-ah)*
l'Irlanda del nord *(leer-lahn-dah)*	**la Carolina del sud** *(kah-roh-lee-nah)*	**i Territori del nord-ovest** *(tehr-ree-toh-ree)*
il Dakota del nord *(dah-koh-tah)*	**il Polo sud** *(poh-loh)*	**il Polo nord** *(poh-loh)*

Le parole italiane per north, south, east **e** west **sono** easy to recognize due to their

similitudini to **inglese.** So . . .

il nord *(nord)*	=	the north	_____
il sud *(sood)*	=	the south	*il sud*
l'est *(lest)*	=	the east	_____
l'ovest *(loh-vest)*	=	the west	_____

del nord	=	northern	_____
del sud	=	southern	_____
dell'est	=	eastern	*dell'est*
dell'ovest	=	western	_____

These **parole sono molto importanti.** Learn them **oggi.** *(oh-jee)* But what about more basic

direzioni *(dee-reh-tsee-oh-nee)* such as "left," "right," **e** "straight ahead"? Let's learn these **parole adesso.**
directions

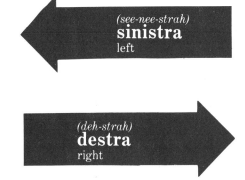

sinistra *(see-nee-strah)*
left

destra *(deh-strah)*
right

straight ahead	=	**diritto** *(dee-reet-toh)*
to the left	=	**a sinistra** *(ah) (see-nee-strah)*
to the right	=	**a destra** *(ah) (deh-strah)*

Just as **in inglese**, these **tre frasi** *(frah-see)* go a long way.

phrases

(pehr) *(fah-voh-reh)* **per favore**	= please	_____
(grah-tsee-eh) **grazie**	= thank you	*grazie, grazie, grazie*
(mee) *(skoo-see)* **mi scusi**	= excuse me	_____

Ecco due conversazioni *(kohn-vehr-sah-tsee-oh-nee)* **tipiche per** someone who is trying to find something.

(tee-pee-keh)

typical

Gianni: **Mi scusi, ma dov'è l'Albergo Florio?**

(mah)

but

Pietro: **Continui diritto, poi giri a sinistra alla seconda strada e l'Albergo Florio è lì a destra.**

(kohn-tee-noo-ee) then *(poh-ee)* *(jee-ree)* turn *(seh-kohn-dah)* second *(strah-dah)* street

(lee) there

Gianni: **Mi scusi, Signore. Dov'è la Villa Giulia?**

Pietro: **Giri qui a destra, continui diritto per cento metri più o meno, e poi giri a sinistra e la Villa Giulia è all'angolo.**

turn *(kwee)* here for *(pehr)* *(meh-tree)* meters *(pee-oo)* more *(meh-noh)* or less

(ahl-lahn-goh-loh) at the corner

Are you lost? There is no need to be lost if **Lei ha** learned the basic **parole di**

(ah) have

direzione. Do not try to memorize these **conversazioni** because you will never be

(dee-reh-tsee-oh-neh) direction

looking for precisely these places. One day you might need to ask for **direzioni** to

"**il Foro Romano**," "**la Torre Pendente**" o "**il Colosseo**." Learn the key **parole**

(foh-roh) the Roman *(roh-mah-noh)* Forum *(tor-reh)* the Leaning Tower *(pen-den-teh)* *(koh-lohs-seh-oh)* the Colosseum

di direzione e be sure **Lei** can find your **destinazione.**

(deh-stee-nah-tsee-oh-neh) destination

What if the person responding to your **domanda** answers too quickly for you to understand

the entire reply? If so, ask again, saying,

☐ **la persona** *(pehr-soh-nah)* .... person _____
☐ **il pezzo** *(peh-tsoh)* .... piece _____
☐ **il piacere** *(pee-ah-cheh-reh)* .... pleasure _____
— **per piacere** .... if you please _____
— **Molto piacere** .... "It's a pleasure to meet you." _____

50

Mi scusi. Sono americano e parlo solamente *(soh-lah-men-teh)* **un poco** *(poh-koh)* **d'italiano. Parli più** *(pee-oo)* **lentamente** *(len-tah-men-teh)*

only little more slowly

per favore, e ripeta la *(lah)* *(soo-ah)* **Sua risposta. Molte grazie.**

your many thanks

Adesso, quando the directions are repeated, **Lei** will be able to understand if **Lei ha** *(leh-ee)* *(ah)*

have

learned the key **parole** for **direzioni.** Quiz yourself by filling in the blanks **sotto con le**

directions

parole corrette in italiano.

Stefano: **Mi scusi, Signorina. Dov'è il ristorante "Alfredo"?** *(ahl-freh-doh)*

Anna: **Da** *(dah)* **qui,** *(kwee)* **continui** _____; **poi, alla terza** *(tehr-zah)* *strada*,

from here straight ahead third street

giri *a* _____. **C'è** *(cheh)* **una chiesa. Subito** *(soo-bee-toh)* **dopo** *(doh-poh)* _____,

right there is immediately after the church

_____ **di** *(dee)* **nuovo** *(noo-oh-voh)* _____ **e il ristorante "Alfredo"**

turn again right

è _____, *all'angolo*. **Buona fortuna.**

on the left on the corner

Ecco quattro verbi nuovi.

aspettare *(ah-spet-tah-reh)* = to wait for *aspettare, aspettare*

capire *(kah-pee-reh)* = to understand _____

vendere *(ven-deh-reh)* = to sell _____

ripetere *(ree-peh-teh-reh)* = to repeat _____

☐ **il piatto** *(pee-aht-toh)* .... plate, dish _____
☐ **la piazza** *(pee-ah-tsah)* .... plaza, town square _____
☐ **la pillola** *(peel-loh-lah)* .... pill _____
☐ **pittoresco** *(peet-toh-reh-skoh)* .... picturesque _____
☐ **la polizia** *(poh-lee-tsee-ah)* .... police _____

51

As always, say each sentence out loud. Say each and every **parola** carefully, pronouncing each Italian sound as well as **Lei** can.

(ah-spet-tah-reh)
aspettare
to wait for

Io *aspetto/* _____ il treno.

Lui
Lei _____ l'autobus.

Noi _____ davanti all'albergo.

Lei _____ il tassì.

Loro _____ (mohl-tee) molti biglietti.
many

(ven-deh-reh)
vendere
to sell

Io _____ dei fiori.

Lui
Lei *vende/* _____ (fruht-tah) della frutta.
fruit

Noi _____ (kahp-poht-toh) un cappotto.
overcoat

Lei _____ una macchina.

Loro _____ (mohlt-tee) molti biglietti.
many

(kah-pee-reh)
capire
to understand

Io *capisco/* _____ l'inglese.

Lui
Lei *capisce/* _____ l'italiano.

Noi *capiamo/* _____ l'italiano.

Lei *capite/* _____ (meh-noo) il menu.
menu

Loro *capiscono/* _____ (roos-soh) il russo.
Russian

(ree-peh-teh-reh)
ripetere
to repeat

Io _____ la parola.

Lui
Lei _____ la risposta.

Noi _____ i nomi.

Lei *ripete/* _____ (leh-tsee-oh-neh) la lezione.
lesson

Loro _____ il verbo.

Adesso, see if **Lei** can translate the following thoughts **in italiano.** **Le risposte sono sotto.**

Note: **Lei** don't need to use these pronouns **in italiano, Lei** can just use **i verbi.**

1. She repeats the word. _____

2. They sell many tickets. _____

3. He waits for the taxi. *Lui aspetta il tassì.*

4. We eat some fruit. _____

5. I speak Italian. _____

6. I drink a cup of tea. _____

52

(dee) (soh-prah) (dee) (soht-toh)
Di Sopra - Di Sotto
above   below

(koh-meen-chah) **(ahn-koh-rah)**
Before **Lei comincia** Step 14, review Step 8. **Adesso impariamo ancora** delle parole.
begin   more

(kah-sah)
Ecco una casa in Italia.

(kah-meh-rah) (let-toh)
La camera da letto è di sopra.

(stahn-zah) (bahn-yoh) (ahn-keh)
La stanza da bagno è anche di sopra.
also

(loof-fee-choh)
L'ufficio è di sotto.

(sah-loht-toh)
Il salotto è anche di sotto.

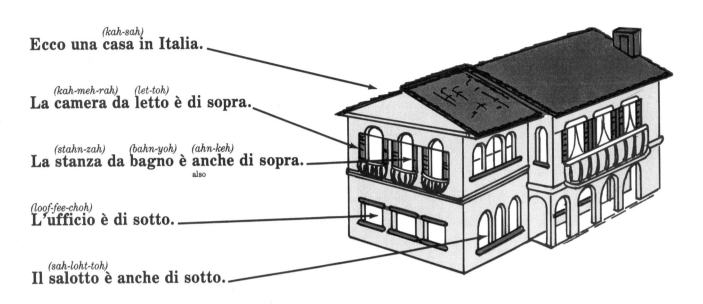

(vah-dah)
Vada adesso in your **camera da letto e** look around **la stanza.** Let's learn **i nomi**
go

delle cose nella camera, just as **abbiamo** learned the various parts of **la casa.** Be sure
of the   in the

to practice saying **le parole** as **Lei** write them in the spaces **sotto.** Also say out loud the

example sentences **sotto le illustrazioni.**

(let-toh)   **(koh-pehr-tah)**   **(koo-shee-noh)**
il letto   **la coperta**   **il cuscino**
                        blanket   pillow

il cuscino

_____   _____
Compro il letto.   **(bee-sohn-yoh)**   **(grahn-deh)**
               Ho bisogno di una coperta.   **Il cuscino è molto grande.**
                   need   big

☐ **la porta** *(pohr-tah)* . . . . door
☐ **il porto** *(pohr-toh)* . . . . port
☐ **la porzione** *(pohr-tsee-oh-neh)* . . . . portion
☐ **possibile** *(pohs-see-bee-leh)* . . . . possible
☐ **la posta** *(poh-stah)* . . . . post office, mail

_____
_____
_____
_____
_____

(zvel-yah)
la sveglia

(lahr-mah-dee-oh)
l'armadio

Remove the next **cinque** stickers **e** label these **cose in** your **camera da letto.**

_____
Ho una sveglia.

(cheh)
C'è un armadio
there is
nella camera.

(oh-stel-loh)
La camera nell'albergo o nell'ostello della
hostel

(joh-ven-too)
gioventù is for sleeping.
youth

(dohr-mee-reh)
dormire = to sleep. This is **un verbo**

(vee-ah-jah-toh-reh) (stahn-koh)
importante per il viaggiatore stanco.
traveler   tired

Study **le domande e le risposte seguenti**

based on **l'illustrazione a sinistra.**

1. Dov'è la sveglia?

   La sveglia è sul tavolo.

2. Dov'è la coperta?

   La coperta è sul letto.

3. Dov'è l'armadio?

   L'armadio è nella camera.

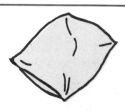

4. Dov'è il cuscino?

   Il cuscino è sul letto.

5. Dov'è il letto?

   Il letto è nella camera.

(grahn-deh)   (peek-koh-loh)
6. Il letto è **grande** o **piccolo?**
   big   small
(nohn)
   Il letto **non** è grande.
   not
   Il letto è piccolo.

☐ **povero** *(poh-veh-roh)* . . . . poor
☐ **precedente** *(preh-cheh-den-teh)* . . . . preceding
☐ **preciso** *(preh-chee-soh)* . . . . precise, exact
  — alle sei preciso . . . . at six o'clock on the dot
☐ **presente** *(preh-sen-teh)* . . . . present

Adesso, risponda alle domande based on the previous **illustrazione.**

Dov'è la sveglia?
(zvel-yah)

La sveglia è _____

Dov'è il letto?

_____

Let's move into **la stanza da bagno e** do the same thing.

(lah-vahn-dee-noh)
il lavandino

il lavandino
_____

C'è un lavandino nella

stanza da bagno.

(doh-chah)
la doccia

_____

La doccia non è nella

camera dell'albergo.

(vee-chee)
il W.C.

_____

Il W.C. non è nella camera
is not

dell'albergo. Il W.C. e la
(kohr-ree-doh-ee-oh)

doccia sono nel **corridoio.**
hallway

(spehk-kee-oh)
lo specchio _____

(ah-shoo-gah-mah-nee)
gli asciugamani *gli asciugamani* _____
towels

(gwahn-toh) *(bahn-yoh)*
il guanto da bagno _____
washglove

(lah-shoo-gah-mah-noh) *(peek-koh-loh)*
l'asciugamano piccolo _____

(bahn-yoh)
l'asciugamano da bagno _____

(grahn-deh)
l'asciugamano grande _____

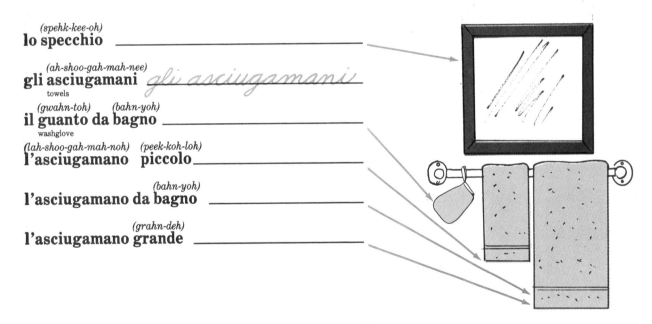

Do not forget to remove **i sette** stickers **seguenti e** label these **cose in** your **stanza da**

bagno.

☐ **prezioso** *(preh-tsee-oh-soh)* .... precious, valuable

☐ **il prezzo** *(preh-tsoh)* .... price

☐ **il problema** *(proh-bleh-mah)* .... problem

☐ **pronto** *(prohn-toh)* .... prompt, ready

—"**Pronto!**" .... "Hello!" (answering telephone)

_____
_____
_____
_____

55

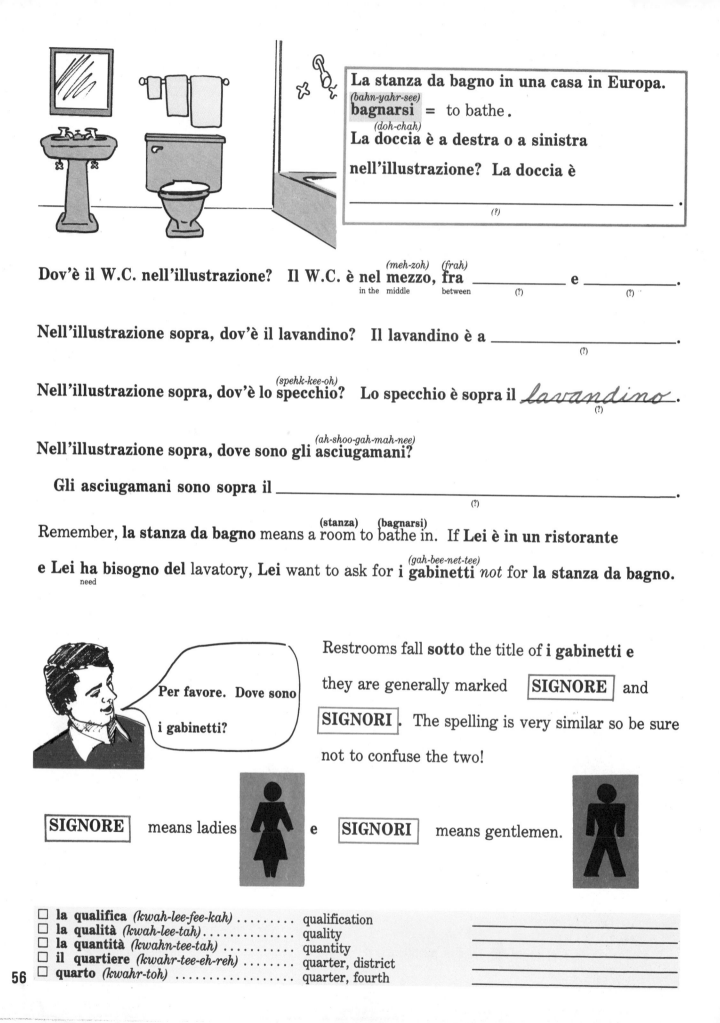

La stanza da bagno in una casa in Europa.
(bahn-yahr-see)
bagnarsi = to bathe.
(doh-chah)
La doccia è a destra o a sinistra

nell'illustrazione? La doccia è

_____ .
(?)

Dov'è il W.C. nell'illustrazione? Il W.C. è nel **mezzo**, **fra** _____ e _____ .
(meh-zoh) *(frah)*
in the middle   between   (?)   (?)

Nell'illustrazione sopra, dov'è il lavandino? Il lavandino è a _____ .
(?)

Nell'illustrazione sopra, dov'è lo **specchio**? Lo specchio è sopra il *lavandino* .
(spehk-kee-oh)   (?)

Nell'illustrazione sopra, dove sono gli **asciugamani**?
(ah-shoo-gah-mah-nee)

Gli asciugamani sono sopra il _____ .
(?)

Remember, **la stanza da bagno** means a room to bathe in. If **Lei è in un ristorante**
(stanza) *(bagnarsi)*

e **Lei ha bisogno del** lavatory, **Lei** want to ask for **i gabinetti** *not* for **la stanza da bagno**.
need   *(gah-bee-net-tee)*

Per favore. Dove sono i gabinetti?

Restrooms fall **sotto** the title of **i gabinetti e** they are generally marked SIGNORE and
SIGNORI . The spelling is very similar so be sure not to confuse the two!

SIGNORE means ladies   e SIGNORI means gentlemen.

Next stop — **l'ufficio,** specifically, **il tavolo** o **la scrivania**
(loof-fee-choh)   _(skree-vah-nee-ah)_
table   desk

nell'ufficio. Che c'è sulla scrivania? Let's identify **le cose** one normally finds
(keh) _(cheh)_
is there

nell'ufficio o strewn about **la casa.**
(oof-fee-choh)

(mah-tee-tah)
la matita

(pen-nah)
la penna

(kahr-tah)
la carta

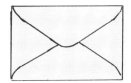
(let-teh-rah)
la lettera

la penna

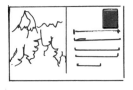
(kahr-toh-lee-nah)
la cartolina

(frahn-koh-bohl-loh)
il francobollo

(lee-broh)
il libro

(ree-vee-stah)
la rivista
magazine

(johr-nah-leh)
il giornale

(ohk-kee-ah-lee)
gli occhiali

(teh-leh-vee-soh-reh)
il televisore

(cheh-stee-noh)
il cestino

57

Adesso, label these **cose nell'ufficio con** your stickers. Do not forget to say these **parole**

out loud whenever **Lei le scrive, Lei** see them **o Lei** apply the stickers. **Adesso,** identify

(leh) (skree-veh)
them write

le cose sotto by filling in each blank **con la parola corretta in italiano.**

1

4

5

6

2

7   IL GIORNALE

8

3   GENTE

9

10

1. _____

2. _____

3. _____

4. _____

5. *la matita*

6. _____

7. _____

8. _____

9. _____

10. _____

Ecco quattro verbi di più.

(dee) (pee-oo)
more

(veh-deh-reh)
vedere = to see

(mahn-dah-reh)
mandare = to send

(dohr-mee-reh)
dormire = to sleep

(troh-vah-reh)
trovare = to find

_____   _____   *dormire*   _____

Adesso, fill in the blanks, **alla prossima pagina, con la forma corretta** of these **verbi.**

(prohs-see-mah)
on   next

Practice saying the sentences out loud many times.

☐ **ricco** *(reek-koh)* . . . . rich

☐ **la ricetta** *(ree-cheht-tah)* . . . . recipe

☐ **il ricordo** *(ree-kohr-doh)* . . . . souvenir, record

☐ **il Rinascimento** *(ree-nah-shee-men-toh)* . . . . . Renaissance

☐ **il rispetto** *(ree-speht-toh)* . . . . respect

(veh-deh-reh)
vedere
to see

Io _vedo_ il letto.

Lui _____ la coperta.
Lei

Noi _____ l'albergo.

Lei _____ il *(koh-lohs-seh-oh)* Colosseo.
Colosseum

Loro _____ la doccia.

(mahn-dah-reh)
mandare
to send

Io _____ la lettera.

Lui _____ la cartolina.
Lei

Noi _____ il libro.

Lei _____ quattro cartoline.

Loro _mandano_ tre lettere.

(dohr-mee-reh)
dormire
to sleep

Io _____ nella camera.

Lui _dorme_ nel letto.
Lei

Noi _____ nell'albergo.

Lei _____ nella casa.

Loro _____ sotto la coperta.

(troh-vah-reh)
trovare
to find

Io _____ il francobollo.

Lui _____ i giornali.
Lei

Noi _troviamo_ gli occhiali.

Lei _____ la *(gohn-doh-lah)* gondola.
Venetian boat

Loro _____ i fiori.

The expressions **"vero"** *(veh-roh)* **o "non è vero"** are useful **in italiano.** When added to the end

of a sentence, the sentence becomes a question for which **la risposta** is usually **"sí."**

Compare them to their equivalents **in inglese.**

È un libro, vero? = It's a book, isn't it?

Sofia è bella, non è vero? = Sophia is beautiful, isn't she?

Lei è italiano, vero? = You're Italian, aren't you?

Mandiamo molte cartoline, non è vero? = We send lots of postcards, don't we?

☐ **il ristorante** *(ree-stoh-rahn-teh)* .... restaurant
☐ **ritardo** *(ree-tahr-doh)* .... late
☐ **la rivista** *(ree-vee-stah)* .... magazine, review
☐ **Roma** *(roh-mah)* .... Rome
☐ **la rosa** *(roh-sah)* .... rose

_____
_____
_____
_____
_____

59

Step 15

Lei know **adesso** how to count, how to ask **domande,** how to use **verbi con** the "plug-in"

formula, how to make statements, **e** how to describe something, be it the location of

un albergo o il colore di una casa. Let's now take the basics that **Lei ha** learned **e**

expand them in special areas that will be most helpful in your travels. What does

everyone do on a holiday? Send postcards, **non è vero?** Let's learn exactly how
(nohn) (eh) (veh-roh)
don't they

l'ufficio postale italiano (PPTT) works.
(loof-fee-choh) (poh-stah-leh)

POSTE

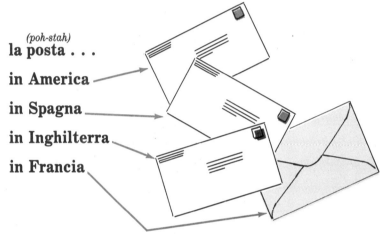

la **posta** . . .
(poh-stah)

in **America**

in **Spagna**

in **Inghilterra**

in **Francia**

The **PPTT** **(Poste e Telegrafi)** is where **Lei** need to go **in Italia** to buy stamps, mail a
(pee-pee-tee-tee) (poh-steh) (teh-leh-grah-fee)
post office

package or send a telegram. **(Lei** may also buy stamps and stationery at the **Sali e**
(sah-lee)

Tabacchi—salt and tobacco store—of which there are many.) **Ecco** some **parole necessarie**
(tah-bahk-kee)

per l'ufficio postale.

la lettera *(let-teh-rah)*	**la cartolina** *(kahr-toh-lee-nah)*	**il francobollo** *(frahn-koh-bohl-loh)*	**il telegramma** *(teh-leh-grahm-mah)*
	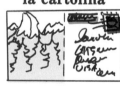		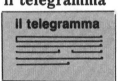

la lettera _____ _____ _____

□ **il sacco** *(sahk-koh)* . . . . sack, bag _____
□ **il sale** *(sah-leh)* . . . . salt _____
　—**Sali e Tabacchi** . . . . salt and tobacco store _____
□ **la salsa** *(sahl-sah)* . . . . sauce _____
60 □ **il saluto** *(sah-loo-toh)* . . . . greeting, salutation _____

(pahk-koh)
il pacco

(boo-kah) (del-leh) (let-teh-reh)
la buca delle lettere

(vee-ah)(ah-eh-reh-ah)
via aerea

(spohr-tel-loh)
lo sportello
ticket window

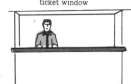

_____   _____   *via aerea*   _____

(kah-bee-nah)(teh-leh-foh-nee-kah)
la cabina telefonica

(teh-leh-foh-noh)
il telefono

(pee-pee-tee-tee) (loof-fee-choh) (poh-stah-leh)
le PPTT /l'ufficio postale

_____   _____   _____

Le PPTT in Italia sono importanti. Lei **manda** *(mahn-dah)* i telegrammi, le lettere, le cartoline
send

e i **pacchi** *(pahk-kee)* dall'ufficio postale. Lei compra i francobolli nell'ufficio postale.

L'ufficio postale è **generalmente** *(jeh-neh-rahl-men-teh)* open from **le 8,00 di mattina alle 2,00 del pomeriggio**

weekdays, **e le 8,00 alle 12,00 il sabato.** *(sah-bah-toh)* **Il Lei ha bisogno** to call home **in America,** this
Saturday

can be done **all'ufficio postale e** is called **una telefonata** *(teh-leh-foh-nah-tah)* **interurbana.** *(een-tair-oor-bah-nah)* (within Italy.)
call   long-distance

Okay. First step — enter **le PPTT.**

The following **è una buona** *(bwoh-nah)* sample **conversazione.** Familiarize yourself **con queste** *(kweh-steh)*
these
parole adesso.

Mi scusi.
Dove si comprano
i francobolli?

Allo sportello
numero 7.

SPORTELLO 7

☐ **la scala** *(skah-lah)* . . . . staircase, stairs   _____
  —la Scala . . . . Milanese opera house   _____
☐ **lo scavo** *(skah-voh)* . . . . excavation   _____
☐ **la scena** *(sheh-nah)* . . . . scene   _____
☐ **la scienza** *(shee-en-zah)* . . . . science   _____

61

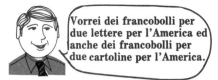  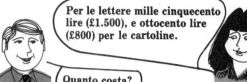

Vorrei dei francobolli per due lettere per l'America ed anche dei francobolli per due cartoline per l'America.

Via aerea?

Per le lettere mille cinquecento lire (£1.500), e ottocento lire (£800) per le cartoline.

Quanto costa?

Sí, via aerea, per favore. Vorrei anche dei francobolli per due lettere per l'Italia. Quanto costa?

Quattrocento lire (£400).

Bene.

Ecco i francobolli. Costano due mila sette cento lire (£2.700).

Molte grazie, Signorina.

Next step — **Lei** ask **domande** like those **sotto** depending upon what **Lei vorrebbe.**
(questions) _(vor-rehb-beh)_ _would like_

Dove compro i francobolli?
I buy

Dove compro una cartolina?

(fah-choh) _(teh-leh-foh-nah-tah)_
Dove faccio una telefonata?
I make _telephone call_

(een-tair-oor-bah-nah)
Dove faccio una telefonata interurbana?

Dov'è l'ufficio postale?

Dove mando un telegramma?
I send

Dove mando un pacco?

Dov'è la cabina telefonica?

Quanto costa?

Dov'è la buca delle lettere?

 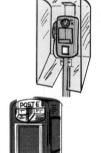

(kwehs-teh)
Ripeta many times **queste frasi di sopra. Adesso,** quiz yourself. See if **Lei** can translate
these

the following thoughts **in italiano. Le risposte sono** at the bottom of **la prossima pagina.**
(prohs-see-mah)
next

1. Where is a telephone booth? _____

2. Where do I make a phone call? _____ _Dove si telefona?_

3. Where is the mailbox? _____

4. Where do I make a long-distance phone call? _____

5. Where is the post office? _____

☐ **secondo** _(seh-kohn-doh)_ .... second _____
☐ **il segnale** _(sen-yah-leh)_ .... signal, sign _____
☐ **il segretario** _(seh-greh-tah-ree-oh)_ ...... secretary _____
☐ **la selezione** _(seh-leh-tsee-oh-neh)_ .... selection, choice _____
62 ☐ **la semisfera** _(seh-mee-sfeh-rah)_ .... hemisphere _____

6. Where does one buy stamps? _____

7. How much is it? _____

8. Where does one send a package? _____

9. Where does one send a telegram? _____

10. Where is window eight? _____

Ecco quattro verbi nuovi.

(fah-reh) **fare** = to do/make   *(moh-strah-reh)* **mostrare** = to show   *(skree-veh-reh)* **scrivere** = to write   *(pah-gah-reh)* **pagare** = to pay

_____   _____   *scrivere*   _____

(fah-reh)
fare
to do/make

Io *faccio/* _____ una telefonata.

Lui *fa/* _____ il letto.
Lei

Noi *facciamo/* _____ molto.

Lei non *fa/* _____ *(nee-ehn-teh)* **niente.**
nothing

Loro *fanno/* _____ *(too-toh)* **tutto.**
everything

(skree-veh-reh)
scrivere
to write

Io _____ una lettera.

Lui *scrive/* _____ **molto.**
Lei   a lot

Noi _____ **un telegramma.**

Lei _____ *(leen-dee-ree-tsoh)* **l'indirizzo.**
address

Loro _____ **niente.**

(moh-strah-reh)
mostrare
to show

Io _____ il libro.

Lui le _____ l'ufficio.
Lei to you

Noi le _____ *(pah-lah-tsoh)* il **palazzo.**
to you

Lei mi *mostra/* _____ la lettera.
to me

Loro mi _____ le PPTT.

(pah-gah-reh)
pagare
to pay

Io _____ *(kohn-toh)* il **conto.**
bill

Lui _____ *(tahs-sah)* la **tassa.**
Lei   tax

Noi *paghiamo/* _____ il giornale.

Lei _____ *(preh-tsoh)* il **prezzo.**
price

Loro non _____ niente.

RISPOSTE

1. Dov'è la cabina telefonica?
2. Dove si telefona?
3. Dov'è la buca delle lettere?
4. Dove si fa una telefonata interurbana?
5. Dov'è l'ufficio postale?
6. Dove si comprano i francobolli?
7. Quanto costa?
8. Dove si manda un pacco?
9. Dove si manda un telegramma?
10. Dov'è lo sportello numero otto?

63

(koh-meh) (pah-gah-reh)
Come Pagare
how   to pay

(chee)
Sì, ci sono anche bills to pay in Italia. Lei have just finished your **pasto** **(pah-stoh)** **squisito** **(skwee-see-toh)**
there are   also   meal   delicious

(vor-rehb-beh)   **(kah-meh-ree-eh-reh)**
e Lei **vorrebbe** il conto e Lei vorrebbe pagare. Che fa Lei? Lei call for **il cameriere**
        would like   waiter

(kah-meh-ree-eh-rah)
o **la cameriera.**
   waitress

Mi scusi. Vorrei il conto, per favore.

Certo, Signore. Un momento.

(kah-meh-ree-eh-reh)
Il cameriere will normally reel off what **Lei**

ha eaten, while writing rapidly. **Lui** will then

(peek-koh-loh)(fohl-yoh)
place **un piccolo foglio di carta sulla**
            little   sheet

tavola that looks like **il conto**

nell'illustrazione, while saying something like:

"Fa tredici mila lire, Signore."
  it makes

(kahs-sah)
Lei will pay **il cameriere** or perhaps **Lei** will pay **alla cassa.** Tipping **in Italia** is the
                                                             cashier's desk

(mahn-chah)
same as tipping **in America.** Generally, **Lei** should leave a 15-percent **mancia sulla tavola.**
                                                              tip

(sehr-vee-tsee-oh)
Sometimes **Lei** will notice that **il servizio** is

included on **il conto,** which means **la mancia**

has already been added on to **il conto** by **il**

ristorante. In this case, **Lei** should not leave

another **mancia.**

(prahn-zoh)
Un pranzo eccellente.
dinner

Grazie.

(preh-goh)
Prego.
you're welcome

(ahr-ree-veh-dehr-chee)
Arrivederci, Signore.
good-bye

☐ **semplice** *(sehm-plee-cheh)* . . . . simple, easy
☐ **il sentimento** *(sen-tee-men-toh)* . . . . feeling
☐ **serio** *(seh-ree-oh)* . . . . serious
☐ **il servizio** *(sehr-vee-tsee-oh)* . . . . service
☐ **sfortunato** *(sfor-too-nah-toh)* . . . . unfortunate

Remember these key **parole** when dining out **all'italiana.** *(ahl-lee-tah-lee-ah-nah)*
in the Italian manner

> *(meh-noo)* *(lee-stah)*
> **il menu** or **la lista**   *(mahn-chah)*
>   **la mancia**
> *(kohn-toh)*
> **il conto**

(jehn-tee-leh-tsah)
La gentilezza è molto importante in Italia. You will feel more **italiano** if you practice
politeness

(kweh-steh) *(es-pres-see-oh-nee)*
and use **queste espressioni.**   **mi scusi**
these   expressions

(pee-ah-cheh-reh)   *(preh-goh)*
per favore or **per piacere**   **grazie** or **molte grazie**   **prego**
                                                                            you're welcome

Ecco una sample **conversazione** involving paying **il conto** when leaving **un albergo.**

Gianni:	**Mi scusi, Signore. Vorrei** *(voh-reh-ee)* **pagare il conto, per favore.**
(lahl-behr-gah-toh-reh) L'albergatore: hotelkeeper	**Che camera, per favore?** *(keh)* what
Gianni:	**Numero trecento dieci.**
L'albergatore:	**Grazie. Un momento, per piacere.**
	Ecco il conto. Fa quindici mila duecento lire.
Gianni:	**Molte grazie (e Gianni** hands him **un biglietto da venti mila lire.** **L'albergatore** returns shortly **e dice.)** *(dee-cheh)* says
L'albergatore:	**Ecco la Sua ricevuta** *(ree-cheh-voo-tah)* **e il resto** *(reh-stoh)* **(4.800 lire). Grazie e arrivederci.** *(ahr-ree-veh-dehr-chee)* your receipt change good-bye

Simple, right? If **Lei ha** any **problema con i numeri,** just ask someone to write out

(sohm-mah)
la somma so that **Lei** can be sure you understand everything correctly.
sum

> *(mee) (skree-vah)*
> **Per favore, mi scriva la somma. Grazie.**
> for me   write   sum

Let's take a break from **il denaro e,** starting **alla prossima pagina,** learn some **nuove** fun
(prohs-see-mah)
next

parole.

- ☐ **sicuro** *(see-koo-roh)* . . . . sure, safe, secure   _____
- ☐ **il sidro** *(see-droh)* . . . . cider   _____
- ☐ **la sigaretta** *(see-gah-ret-tah)* . . . . cigarette   _____
- ☐ **il sigaro** *(see-gah-roh)* . . . . cigar   _____
- ☐ **simile** *(see-mee-leh)* . . . . similar   _____   65

È in buona salute. *(sah-loo-teh)* health

È malato. *(mah-lah-toh)* sick

È buono. *(bwoh-noh)* good

Non è buono.

È cattivo. *(kaht-tee-voh)* bad

L'acqua è calda. *(kahl-dah)* warm

Sono 50 gradi.

L'acqua è fredda. *(frehd-dah)* cold

Sono 17 gradi.

50°

17°

FORTE!

piano

Lei parla forte. *(for-teh)* loudly

Noi parliamo piano. *(pee-ah-noh)* softly

La linea rossa è corta. *(kohr-tah)* short

La linea azzurra è lunga. *(loon-gah)* long

La donna è grande. *(grahn-deh)*

Il bambino è piccolo. *(peek-koh-loh)*

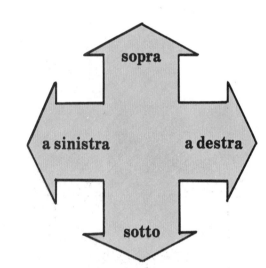

sopra

a sinistra   a destra

sotto

Il libro rosso è grosso. *(grohs-soh)* thick

Il libro verde è sottile. *(soht-tee-leh)* thin

20 chilometri all'ora *(kee-loo-meh-tree)* per hour

200 chilometri all'ora

lento *(len-toh)* slow

veloce / rapido *(veh-loh-cheh)(rah-pee-doh)* fast

(mohn-tahn-yeh)   *(ahl-teh)*

Le montagne sono alte. **Sono alte 2000 metri.**
<u>high</u>   *(meh-tree)* meters

(bahs-seh)   *(soh-lah-men-teh)*

Le montagne sono basse. **Sono alte solamente 800 metri.**
<u>low</u>   only

(vek-kee-oh) *(ah)*   *(ahn-nee)*

Il nonno è vecchio. **Ha settanta anni.**
<u>old</u> he has years

(joh-vah-neh)

Il bambino è giovane. **Ha solamente dieci anni.**
<u>young</u>

(kah-rah)

La camera dell'albergo è cara. **Costa 50.000 lire.**
<u>expensive</u>

(oh-stehl-loh) *(joh-ven-too)* *(eh-koh-noh-mee-kah)*

La camera dell'ostello della gioventù è economica.
hostel   youth   <u>inexpensive</u>

Costa 5.000 lire.

PENSIONE

(reek-koh) *(mohl-toh)*

Ho 500.000 lire. Sono ricco. È molto denaro.
<u>rich</u> <u>much</u>

(poh-veh-roh) *(poh-koh)*

Lui ha solamente 200 lire. È povero. È poco denaro.
<u>poor</u> <u>little</u>

£200

£500.000

(deh-ee)

Ecco dei verbi nuovi.
some

(sah-peh-reh)

sapere = to know
(a fact, an
address, etc.)

(poh-teh-reh)

potere = to be
able to/can

(doh-veh-reh)

dovere = to have to/
to owe

(leh-jeh-reh)

leggere = to read

_____   _____   *dovere*   _____

I verbi "sapere," "potere," "dovere," along with **"volere,"** can be joined with another

verbo:

Sappiamo trovare l'indirizzo.
we know how to find the address

Sappiamo parlare italiano.

Possiamo parlare.
we can speak

Possiamo capire.
understand

Dobbiamo pagare.
we must pay

Dobbiamo mangiare.
eat

☐ **la sorpresa** *(sohr-preh-sah)* . . . . surprise
☐ **lo spagnolo** *(spahn-yoh-loh)* . . . . Spanish, Spaniard
☐ **lo spettacolo** *(speht-tah-koh-loh)* . . . . spectacle, show
☐ **gli Stati Uniti** *(stah-tee)* *(oo-nee-tee)* . . . . . . United States
☐ **lo straniero** *(strah-nee-eh-roh)* . . . . stranger, foreigner

_____
_____
_____
_____
_____

Study their pattern closely as **Lei** will use **molto questi verbi.**
(kweh-stee)
a lot   these

(sah-peh-reh)
sapere
to know

Io ___so/___ tutto.
everything

Lui ___sa/___ l'indirizzo.
Lei

Noi ___sappiamo/___ parlare italiano.

Lei ___sa/___ ordinare una birra.

Loro ___sanno/___ l'indirizzo.

(poh-teh-reh)
potere
to be able to/can

Io ___posso/___ parlare italiano.

Lui ___può/___ capire l'inglese.
Lei

Noi ___possiamo/___ bere.

Lei ___può/___ entrare.

Loro ___possono/___ parlare italiano anche.

(doh-veh-reh)
dovere
to have to/owe

Io ___devo/___ pagare il conto.

Lui ___deve/___ restare all'albergo.
Lei

Noi ___dobbiamo/___ visitare Roma.
(vee-see-tah-reh)
to visit

(chee)
Lei ci ___deve/___ 100 lire.
to us

Loro ___devono/___ pagare il conto.

(leh-jeh-reh)
leggere
to read

Io _____ il libro.

Lui _____ il giornale.
Lei

Noi ___leggiamo/___ la lista.

Lei _____ molto.

Loro _____ tutto.

(pwah)
Può Lei translate these thoughts **sotto in italiano? Le risposte sono sotto.**
can

1. I can speak Italian. _____

2. He must pay now. _____

3. We don't know the address. _____

4. You owe us 10,000 lire. *Lei ci deve dieci mila lire.*

5. She knows everything. _____

6. I am able to speak Italian. _____

68

Adesso, draw **delle linee** *(lee-neh)* **fra** the opposites **sotto.** Don't forget to say them out loud.

Use **queste parole** *(kweh-steh)* every day to describe **le cose nella Sua casa,** *(soo-ah)* **nella Sua scuola,** *(skoo-oh-lah)* at
these   your   school

work, etc.

(grahn-deh)
grande

(ah) *(see-nee-strah)*
a sinistra

(joh-vah-neh)
giovane

(poh-veh-roh)
povero

(een) (bwoh-nah)(sah-loo-teh)
in buona salute

(loon-goh)
lungo

(mohl-toh)
molto

(bwoh-noh)
buono

(grohs-soh)
grosso

(ahl-toh)
alto

(kahl-doh)
caldo

(soht-toh)
sotto

(pee-ah-noh)
piano

(kah-roh)
caro

(len-toh)
lento

(soh-prah)
sopra

(bahs-soh)
basso

(peek-koh-loh)
piccolo

(for-teh)
forte

(soht-tee-leh)
sottile

(eh-koh-noh-mee-koh)
economico

(poh-koh)
poco

(mah-lah-toh)
malato

(vek-kee-oh)
vecchio

(veh-loh-cheh)(rah-pee-doh)
veloce / rapido

(ah)(deh-strah)
a destra

(frehd-doh)
freddo

(reek-koh)
ricco

(kaht-tee-voh)
cattivo

(kor-toh)
corto

☐ **straordinario** *(strah-ohr-dee-nah-ree-oh)* . . . extraordinary
☐ **lo studio** *(stoo-dee-oh)* . . . . study, studio
☐ **il successo** *(soo-chehs-soh)* . . . . success
☐ **sud** *(sood)* . . . . south
☐ **superiore** *(soo-peh-ree-oh-reh)* . . . . superior, above

Step 17

Il Viaggiatore Viaggia
(vee-ah-jah-toh-reh) traveler *(vee-ah-jah)* travels

Ieri a Venezia! **Oggi a Milano!** **Domani a Bologna!**

Lunedì a Firenze! **Mercoledì a Napoli!** **Venerdì a Brindisi!**

Traveling **è** easy and quite efficient **in Italia. L'Italia non è grande,** therefore **il**

viaggio è molto facile within the distinctive "boot" **che si chiama "l'Italia."**
(fah-chee-leh) easy *(keh)* that *(see)* is *(kee-ah-mah)* called

Come viaggiare in Italia?
(vee-ah-jah-reh) travel

Stefano viaggia in macchina.   **Franca viaggia in treno.**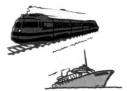

Francesca viaggia in aereo.   **Anna viaggia in nave.**
(nah-veh) ship

Andrea e Silvia viaggiano in bicicletta attraverso l'Italia.
(aht-trah-vehr-soh) across

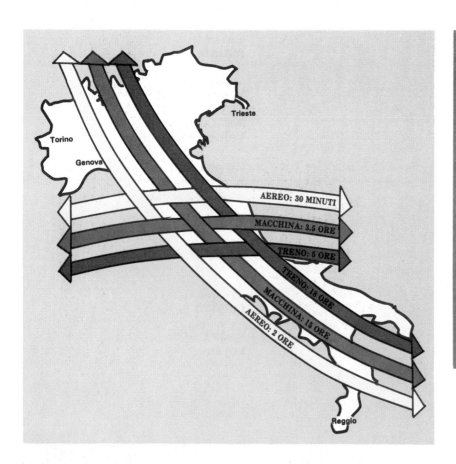

AEREO: 30 MINUTI
MACCHINA: 3.5 ORE
TRENO: 5 ORE
TRENO: 18 ORE
MACCHINA: 15 ORE
AEREO: 2 ORE

Torino · Genova · Trieste · Reggio

Guardi la carta
(goo-ahr-dee) look at

geografica a sinistra.

È l'Italia, non è vero?
isn't it

Per viaggiare dal nord al

sud in aereo, ci vogliono
(chee) it *(vohl-yah-noh)* takes

solamente due ore,

15 ore in macchina, 18 ore

in treno. Non c'è
not bad, *(cheh)*

male, vero?
is it

☐ **il tabacco** *(tah-bahk-koh)* .... tobacco
☐ **il tassì** *(tahs-see)* .... taxi
☐ **il tavolo** *(tah-voh-loh)* .... table
  —la tavola calda .... cafeteria
☐ **il teatro** *(teh-ah-troh)* .... theater

Gli Italiani enjoy going on **vacanze,** *(vah-kahn-tseh)* so it is no **sorpresa** *(sohr-preh-sah)* to find **molte parole** built on **la**

parola "viaggiare," *(vee-ah-jah-reh)* which means "to travel." Practice saying **le parole seguenti** many

times. **Lei** will use them **spesso.** *(spehs-soh)* often

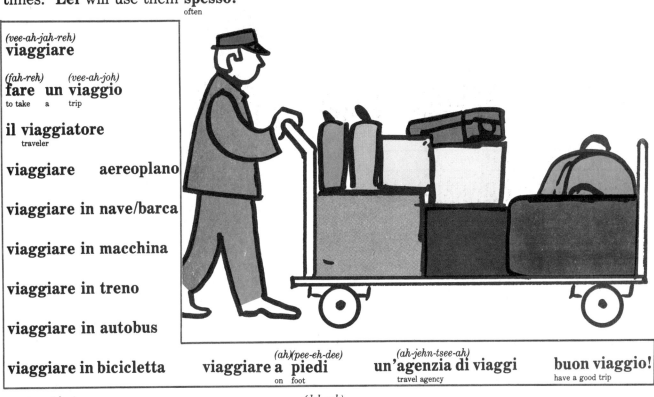

(vee-ah-jah-reh)
viaggiare

(fah-reh) *(vee-ah-joh)*
fare un viaggio
to take a trip

il viaggiatore
traveler

viaggiare aereoplano

viaggiare in nave/barca

viaggiare in macchina

viaggiare in treno

viaggiare in autobus

viaggiare in bicicletta **viaggiare a piedi** *(ah)(pee-eh-dee)* on foot **un'agenzia di viaggi** *(ah-jehn-tsee-ah)* travel agency **buon viaggio!** have a good trip

Sotto ci sono *(chee)* some basic signs which **Lei deve** *(deh-veh)* should also learn to recognize quickly. Most of

queste parole *(kwes-teh)* come from **i verbi** **entrare** *(en-trah-reh)* e **uscire** *(oos-chee-reh)* = to go out.

(len-trah-tah) *(leen-gres-soh)*
l'entrata or **l'ingresso** _____
entrance   entrance

(preen-chee-pah-leh)
l'entrata principale _____
main entrance

(lah-teh-rah-leh)
l'entrata laterale _____
side entrance

(loo-shee-tah)
l'uscita _*l'uscita*_
exit

l'uscita principale _____
main exit

(see-koo-reh-tsah)
l'uscita di sicurezza _____
emergency exit

(vee-eh-tah-toh)
vietato l'ingresso _____
do not enter

L'USCITA

L'ENTRATA

L'INGRESSO

☐ **il telefono** *(teh-leh-foh-noh)* . . . . telephone   _____
☐ **il telegramma** *(teh-leh-grahm-mah)* . . . . telegram   _____
☐ **il televisore** *(teh-leh-vee-soh-reh)* . . . . television set   _____
☐ **la temperatura** *(tem-peh-rah-too-rah)* . . . . . . temperature   _____
☐ **il Tevere** *(teh-veh-reh)* . . . . Tiber River   _____

71

(ahn-dah-reh)
Andare è un verbo molto importante per il **viaggiatore.** *(vee-ah-jah-toh-reh)* If you choose to **andare in**
to go   traveler

macchina, here are a few key **parole.**

(lah-oo-toh-strah-dah)
l'autostrada   *l'autostrada*
highway

(strah-dah)
la strada per Verona _____
road   to   Verona

(ah-jehn-tsee-ah) (noh-leh-joh)
un'agenzia di noleggio _____
car rental agency

(kohn-trahv-ven-tsee-oh-neh)   *(mool-tah)*
una contravvenzione or **una multa** _____
traffic ticket   traffic fine

(mahk-kee-nah)   *(noh-leh-jah-reh)*
una macchina da noleggiare _____
rental car

Ecco quattro opposites **molto importanti.**

Milano-**Bologna-Prato-Firenze**-Roma

(lahr-ree-voh)
l'arrivo _____
arrival

(pahr-ten-tsah)
la partenza   *la partenza*
departure

(een-tair-nah-tsee-oh-nahl-ee)
internazionale _____
international

(nah-tsee-oh-nahl-ee)
nazionale _____
domestic

Let's learn the basic **verbi di viaggio.** *(vee-ah-joh)* Follow the same pattern you have in previous Steps.

(vee-ah-jah-reh)
viaggiare = to travel

(aht-tehr-rah-reh)
atterrare = to land

(preh-noh-tah-reh)
prenotare = to reserve/to book

atterrare

(ahr-ree-vah-reh)
arrivare = to arrive

(pahr-tee-reh)
partire = to leave

(gwee-dah-reh)
guidare = to drive (cars)

(sah-lee-reh)
salire = to board/
to climb into

(shen-deh-reh)
scendere = to get out/
go down

(kahm-bee-ah-reh)
cambiare (treno) = to
transfer (trains)

(ahn-dah-reh) (ah-air-ee-oh)
andare in aereo = to go by plane/fly

☐ **il terrazzo** *(tehr-rah-tsoh)* . . . . terrace   _____
☐ **il tesoro** *(teh-soh-roh)* . . . . treasure   _____
☐ **il titolo** *(tee-toh-loh)* . . . . title   _____
☐ **la torre** *(tohr-reh)* . . . . tower   _____
   —La Torre Pendente . . . . Leaning Tower (of Pisa)   _____

Con questi verbi, Lei è ready for any **viaggio** *(vee-ah-joh)* anywhere. **Lei** should have no **problemi con i verbi.** Just remember the basic "plug-in" formula **noi** learned already. Use that knowledge to translate the following thoughts **in italiano. Le risposte sono sotto.**

1. I fly (go by plane) to Rome. _____

2. I transfer trains in Milan._____

3. He lands in Paris. _____

4. We arrive tomorrow. _____

5. You get out in Florence. _____

6. They travel to Rome. _____

7. Where is the train to Padua? _____

8. How can one fly (go by plane) to Switzerland? With Pan Am or Alitalia?_____

_____

Ecco alcune parole nuove per il *(ahl-koo-neh)* **Suo viaggio.** *(soo-oh)* As always, write out **le parole e** practice the sample **frasi** *(frah-see)* out loud.
some   your
sentences

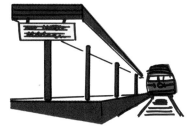

(mahr-chah-pee-eh-deh) *(bee-nah-ree-oh)*
il marciapiede e il binario
platform   train track

(stah-tsee-oh-neh)
la stazione dei treni
train station

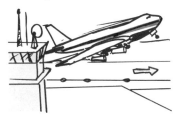

(lah-air-ee-oh-pohr-toh)
l'aereoporto
airport

_____

_____

l'aereoporto

Mi scusi. Dov'è il binario numero due?

Mi scusi. Dov'è la stazione dei treni?

Mi scusi. Dov'è l'aereoporto?

73

(loof-fee-choh) *(kahm-bee-oh)*
l'ufficio di cambio
money-exchange office

———————————————

Mi scusi. Dov'è
l'ufficio di cambio?

(oh-jet-tee) *(smah-ree-tee)*
ufficio oggetti smarriti
lost-and-found office

UFFICIO OGGETTI SMARRITI

———————————————

Mi scusi. Dov'è l'ufficio
oggetti smarriti?

(loh-rah-ree-oh) *(fehr-roh-vee-eh)*
l'orario delle ferrovie
timetable   railroad

———————————————

Mi scusi. Dov'è l'orario?

(ohk-koo-pah-toh)
occupato ——————————————
occupied
(lee-beh-roh)
libero ——————————————
free
(skohm-pahr-tee-men-toh)
lo scompartimento ——————————
compartment
(poh-stoh)
il posto _____ *il posto*
seat
(kweh-stoh)
Questo posto è occupato? ——————
this   is

Questo posto è libero? ——————————

(skohm-pahr-tee-men-toh)
Questo scompartimento è occupato? ————

Questo scompartimento è libero? ————

(pee-oo)(tahr-dee)
Practice writing out **le domande seguenti.** It will help you **più tardi.**
later

Mi scusi. Dove sono i gabinetti? ——————————————————

(vah-goh-neh)(ree-stoh-rahn-teh)
Mi scusi. Dov'è il vagone ristorante? ——————————————
dining car
(sah-lah) *(dah-spet-toh)*
Dov'è la sala d'aspetto? _*Dov'è la sala d'aspetto?*_
waiting room
(spohr-tel-loh)
Dov'è lo sportello numero otto? ——————————————

(vee-eh-tah-toh)(foo-mah-reh)
È vietato fumare? ——————————————————
is it prohibited   to smoke

———

- ☐ **il tram** *(trahm)* . . . . tram, street car ——————————
- ☐ **tranquillo** *(trahn-kweel-loh)* . . . . calm, tranquil ——————————
- ☐ **tre** *(treh)* . . . . three ——————————
- ☐ **il treno** *(treh-noh)* . . . . train ——————————
74 ☐ **il turista** *(too-ree-stah)* . . . . tourist ——————————

Increase your **parole di viaggio** *(vee-ah-joh)* by writing out **le parole sotto e** practicing the **frasi** *(frah-see)* sentences

out loud.

per *(pehr)* _____
for/to   Dov'è il treno per Roma?

tempo *(tem-poh)* _____
time   Ho molto poco tempo.

il binario *(bee-nah-ree-oh)* _____
track   Il treno parte dal binario numero tre.

ufficio informazioni *(een-for-mah-tsee-oh-nee)* _____
information office

l'ufficio deposito bagagli *(deh-poh-see-toh) (bah-gahl-yee)* _____
left-luggage office

_____
Dov'è l'ufficio deposito bagagli?

il facchino *(fahk-kee-noh)* _____
porter

il biglietto *(beel-yet-toh)* *il biglietto*
airplane/train ticket

Practice **queste parole** every day. **Lei** will be surprised how **spesso Lei** *(spehs-soh)* will use them.
often

Può Lei leggere la lezione seguente? *(poo-oh)*
can

Lei è adesso seduto *(seh-doo-toh)* **nell'aereoplano e va in Italia. Lei ha** exchanged **il denaro** (you have, seated

haven't you?). **Lei ha i biglietti e il passaporto** *(pahs-sah-pohr-toh)* **e ha i bagagli** *(bah-gahl-yee)* all packed. **Adesso, è un** bags/suitcases

turista. Lei atterra *(aht-tehr-rah)* **domani alle 14,15 in Italia. Buon viaggio! Buon divertimento!**

Adesso, Lei have arrived **e Lei** head for **la stazione** in order to get to **la Sua destinazione** *(deh-stee-nah-tsee-oh-neh)*
destination

finale. *(fee-nah-leh)* As **Lei** know, **i treni italiani** come in varying speeds: **il rapido** *(rah-pee-doh)* **e l'espresso**

(molto rapidi); il diretto *(dee-ret-toh)* **e il direttissimo** *(dee-ret-tees-see-moh)* **(rapidi); e l'accelerato** *(lah-cheh-leh-rah-toh)* **(lento).** Some

treni hanno il vagone *(ahn-noh) (vah-goh-neh)* **ristorante** *(ree-stoh-rahn-teh)* **e** some **treni hanno il vagone letto** *(let-toh)* **o le cuccette.** *(koo-chet-teh)*
have   dining car   sleeping car   berths

All this will be indicated **sull'orario,** but remember **Lei sa come** to ask things like this.

Practice your possible **combinazioni di domande** *(kohm-bee-nah-tsee-oh-nee)* by writing out the following samples.
combinations

C'è un vagone ristorante sul treno? *(cheh)* _____
is there
Ci sono delle cuccette sul treno? *(chee) (koo-chet-teh)* _____

C'è un vagone letto sul treno? _____

□ **l'ufficio** *(loof-fee-choh)* .... office   _____
□ **ultimo** *(ool-tee-moh)* .... final, last, ultimate   _____
□ **unico** *(oo-nee-koh)* .... unique, only, single   _____
  —senso unico .... one-way (traffic sign)   _____
□ **universale** *(oo-nee-vehr-sah-leh)* .... universal

What about inquiring about **il** **prezzo** *(preh-tsoh)* price **dei biglietti** *(beel-yet-tee)* **o la tariffa?** *(tah-reef-fah)* fare . **Lei può fare** *(fah-reh)* make **delle** some

domande.

(kwahn-toh)
Quanto è il biglietto (la tariffa) per Taranto?_____

semplice *(sem-plee-cheh)* one-way _____*semplice*_____   **andata e ritorno** *(ahn-dah-tah) (ree-tohr-noh)* round-trip _____

Quanto è il biglietto per Siena? *(see-eh-nah)*_____

Quanto è il biglietto per Bari? *(bah-ree)*_____

Semplice o andata e ritorno? *(sem-plee-cheh)* _____

What about times of **partenze e arrivi?** *(pahr-ten-tseh)* departures *(ahr-ree-vee)* arrivals   **Lei può fare queste domande anche.**

A che ora parte il treno per Belluno? leaves _____*a che*_____

A che ora parte l'aereoplano per Roma?_____

A che ora arriva il treno da Parigi? *(pah-ree-jee)* from _____

A che ora arriva il volo *(voh-loh)* flight **da Nuova York?** _____

Lei have arrived in **Italia.** **Lei è adesso alla stazione.** **Dove vorrebbe andare?** *(vohr-rehb-beh)* would you like Well,

tell that to **la persona** at the **sportello** selling **i biglietti.** *(beel-yet-tee)*

Vorrei andare in Francia. *(frahn-chah)*_____

Vorrei andare a Rimini. *(ree-mee-nee)* _____

Vorremmo andare a Ravenna. *(rah-ven-nah)* *Vorremmo andare a Ravenna.*

A che ora parte il treno per Napoli? *(nah-poh-lee)* _____

Quanto costa il biglietto per Catanzaro? *(kah-tahn-zah-roh)*_____

Vorrei un biglietto per Lecce. *(leh-cheh)*_____

prima classe *(pree-mah) (klahs-seh)* first class _____   **seconda classe** *(seh-kohn-dah)* second class _____

Semplice o andata e ritorno? _____

Devo cambiare treno? *(deh-voh)* must I _____ **Grazie.**_____

Con this practice, **Lei è** off **e** running. **Queste parole di viaggio** will make your holiday

twice as enjoyable **e** at least three times as easy. Review **queste parole nuove** by doing

76 the crossword puzzle **alla pagina** 77. Practice drilling yourself on this Step by selecting

other locations **e** asking your own **domande** about **i treni, gli autobus o gli aereoplani**
(l-yee)

that go there. Select **parole nuove dal Suo dizionario e** practice asking questions
(soo-oh)
your

that **cominciano con**
(koh-meen-chah-noh)
begin

| DOVE | QUANDO | QUANTO | QUANTE VOLTE |

QUANTE VOLTE *(vohl-teh)* how often/how many times

o making statements like

Vorrei andare a Roma.

Vorrei comprare un biglietto.

PAROLE CROCIATE
(kroh-chah-teh)

ACROSS

1. lease/rent
2. have a good trip
3. to smoke
4. occupied
5. timetable
6. money
7. foreign
8. flight
9. nothing
10. time
11. to board/to climb into
12. to leave
13. arrival
14. entrance
15. station
16. to reserve
17. to get out/go down
18. domestic

DOWN

1. we/us
2. to drive
3. information office
4. prohibited
5. track
6. exit
7. train
8. to fly/go by plane
9. ticket window
10. free
11. traveler
12. passport
13. departure

GUIDARE

Step 18

Il Menu o la Lista
(meh-noo) *(lee-stah)*
menu

Lei è adesso in Italia e Lei ha una camera. E adesso? Lei ha fame. *(fah-meh)* **Vorrebbe mangiare.** *(mahn-jah-reh)*
have hunger you would like

Ma, dov'è un buon ristorante? *(mah)* but First of all, **ci sono** *(chee)* different types of places to eat.

Let's learn them.

il ristorante *(ree-stoh-rahn-teh)*	=	exactly what it says, with a variety of meals and prices
la trattoria *(traht-toh-ree-ah)*	=	usually less elegant and less expensive than a **ristorante,** often run by a family
l'osteria *(loh-steh-ree-ah)*	=	found in the country or in small towns, serves mostly drinks and easy-to-prepare food
la tavola calda *(tah-voh-lah)(kahl-dah)*	=	similar to a cafeteria, serving a variety of foods (You may eat sitting down or standing up.)
il bar *(bahr)*	=	serves pastries and sandwiches, concentrates on liquid refreshments (great place for morning coffee or tea)

Try them all. Experiment. **Adesso Lei trova un buon ristorante. Entra nel ristorante e trova un posto.** seat Sharing **tavole con** others **è** a common **e molto** pleasant **costume in** *(koh-stoo-meh)* custom **Europa.** If **Lei vede una sedia** *(veh-deh)* see vacant, just be sure to ask

Mi scusi. Questo posto è libero? *(lee-beh-roh)*

If **Lei ha bisogno di una lista,** need catch the attention of **il cameriere e** *(kah-meh-ree-eh-reh)* say

Cameriere! La lista, per favore.

☐ **l'università** *(loo-nee-vehr-see-tah)* . . . . . . university
☐ **urbano** *(oor-bah-noh)* . . . . urban
☐ **usato** *(oo-sah-toh)* . . . . used, second-hand
☐ **usuale** *(oo-soo-ah-leh)* . . . . usual, customary
☐ **l'utensile** *(loo-ten-see-leh)* . . . . utensil

78

In Italia, ci sono tre main **pasti** *(pah-stee)* to enjoy every day, plus **un caffè** *(kahf-feh)* e perhaps **un dolce** *(dohl-cheh)* per
meals   pastry

(vee-ah-jah-toh-reh)(stahn-koh)   *(poh-meh-ree-joh)*
il viaggiatore stanco late in **il pomeriggio.**
traveler   tired

(koh-lah-tsee-oh-neh) **la colazione** or **la prima colazione**	= breakfast . . . This is a "continental breakfast" with **caffè o tè e pane** or a sweet roll. Be sure to check serving times before retiring.
(prahn-zoh) **il pranzo**	= lunch . . . . . . This is the big meal of the day. It usually includes a pasta dish or soup, an entree and salad. It is generally served from noon to 14:00.
(cheh-nah) **la cena**	= dinner . . . . . This is a light meal often consisting of soup, cheese or eggs. It is generally served from 19:30 to 22:00.

If **Lei** look around you **nel ristorante italiano, Lei** will see that some **costumi italiani** *(koh-stoo-mee)*
customs

(deef-feh-ren-tee)   *(pah-neh)*
sono differenti from ours. **Il pane** may be set directly on the tablecloth, elbows are

often rested **sulla tavola** and please do not forget to mop up your **sugo con il Suo pane!** *(soo-goh)*
sauce

Lei will hear **"Buon appetito!"** *(bwohn) (ahp-peh-tee-toh)* before **il Suo pasto e** an inquiring **"Ha mangiato bene?"** *(ah) (mahn-jah-toh) (beh-neh)*
did you eat   well

after **Lei** have finished. **Il cameriere** is asking if **Lei** enjoyed **il Suo pasto e** if it tasted

good. A smile **e a "Sí, grazie"** will tell him that you enjoyed it.

Adesso, it may be **prima colazione** *(koh-lah-tsee-oh-neh)* time **a Denver, ma Lei è in Italia e sono le 19,00.**
but

Many **ristoranti italiani** post **la lista** outside. Always read it before entering so **Lei**

sa what type of **pasto e prezzo** *(preh-tsoh)* **Lei** will encounter inside. Most **ristoranti** offer
price

(pee-aht-toh) (johr-noh)   *(preh-tsoh)*
il piatto del giorno o una lista a prezzo fisso. These are complete **pasti** at fair **prezzi.**
special meal of the day   fixed

In addition, **ci sono** all the following main categories **sulla lista.**

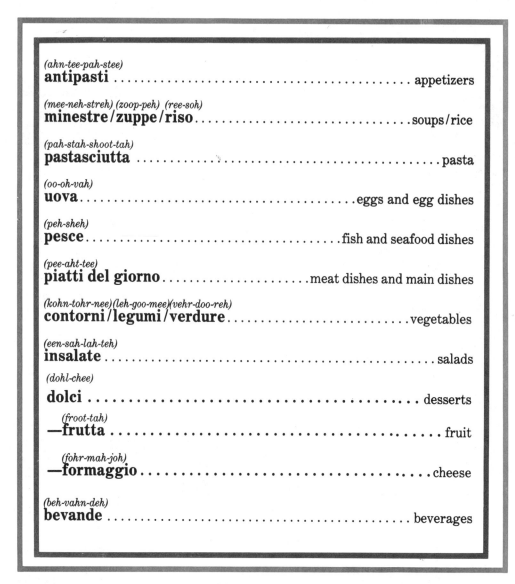

(ahn-tee-pah-stee)
antipasti . . . . appetizers

(mee-neh-streh) (zoop-peh) (ree-soh)
minestre/zuppe/riso . . . . soups/rice

(pah-stah-shoot-tah)
pastasciutta . . . . pasta

(oo-oh-vah)
uova . . . . eggs and egg dishes

(peh-sheh)
pesce . . . . fish and seafood dishes

(pee-aht-tee)
piatti del giorno . . . . meat dishes and main dishes

(kohn-tohr-nee)(leh-goo-mee)(vehr-doo-reh)
contorni/legumi/verdure . . . . vegetables

(een-sah-lah-teh)
insalate . . . . salads

(dohl-chee)
dolci . . . . desserts

(froot-tah)
—frutta . . . . fruit

(fohr-mah-joh)
—formaggio . . . . cheese

(beh-vahn-deh)
bevande . . . . beverages

Most **ristoranti** also offer **le specialità della casa o** special meals prepared **dal cuoco.**
(speh-chah-lee-tah) specialties / *(koo-oh-koh)* cook

And if **Lei** are sampling **il vino,** don't forget to ask about the **vino della casa. Adesso**
house wine

for a preview of delights to come . . . At the back of this **libro, Lei trova** a sample

lista italiana. Legga la lista oggi e impari le parole nuove! Quando Lei are ready
(oh-jee)

to leave for **Europa,** cut out **la lista,** fold it **e** carry it in your pocket, wallet **o**

purse. **Lei può andare in** any **ristorante e** feel prepared. (May we suggest studying **la lista**
(poo-oh) can

after, **e** not before, **Lei ha** eaten!)

☐ **la varietà** *(vah-ree-eh-tah)* . . . . variety
☐ **il vaso** *(vah-soh)* . . . . vase
☐ **la vena** *(veh-nah)* . . . . vein
☐ **il venditore** *(vehn-dee-toh-reh)* . . . . vendor, seller
☐ **la versione** *(vehr-see-oh-neh)* . . . . version

In addition, learning the following should help **Lei** to identify what kind of meat **o** poultry

Lei ordina e come it will be prepared.
    order   how

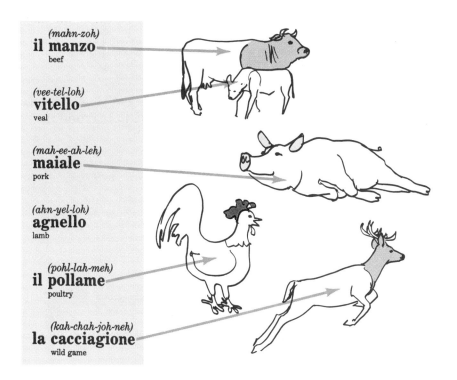

(mahn-zoh)
il manzo
beef

(vee-tel-loh)
vitello
veal

(mah-ee-ah-leh)
maiale
pork

(ahn-yel-loh)
agnello
lamb

(pohl-lah-meh)
il pollame
poultry

(kah-chah-joh-neh)
la cacciagione
wild game

(koht-toh)
cotto = cooked

(ahr-roh-stoh)
arrosto = roasted

(freet-toh)
fritto = fried

(ahl) (fohr-noh)
al forno = baked

(greel-yah)
alla griglia = grilled

(fahr-chee-toh)
farcito = stuffed

               (vehr-doo-reh)   *(vehr-deh)*
Lei will also get **verdure con il Suo pasto** and perhaps **un'insalata verde.** One day at an
                 vegetables   green

(mehr-kah-toh)   *(froot-tah)*
open-air **mercato** will teach you **i nomi** for all the different kinds of **verdure e frutta,**
       market

plus it will be a delightful experience for you. **Lei può** always consult your menu guide at
                                           can

                            (dee-men-tee-kah)
the back of **questo libro** if **Lei dimentica il nome corretto. Adesso Lei ha** decided what
                                  forget

(vor-rehb-beh)
Lei vorrebbe mangiare e il cameriere arriva.

E come bevanda?

Vorrei i ravioli e la costoletta di vitello.

Un bicchiere di vino bianco, per piacere.

☐ **la vergine** *(vehr-jee-neh)* . . . . virgin
  —**la Santa Vergine** . . . . Holy Virgin
☐ **la via** *(vee-ah); via* . . . . way; by
  —**via Appia Antica** . . . . Appian Way
  —**via aerea** . . . . by air, airmail

81

Non si dimentichi *(see) (dee-men-tee-kee)* to treat yourself to **un dolce italiano.** *(dohl-cheh)* **Lei** would not want to miss out **on**
don't forget

trying **i dolci seguenti.**

(krehm)
una crème caramel
custard with burnt sugar sauce

(kahn-noh-lee)
cannoli
pastries filled with sweetened ricotta cheese

(grah-nee-tah)
granita
ice with fruit syrup or coffee

(zah-bahl-yoh-neh)
zabaglione
custard of eggs, sugar and wine

After completing **il Suo pasto,** call **il cameriere e** pay just as **Lei ha** already learned in

Step 16:

Cameriere, vorrei il conto, per favore.

Sotto c'è una *(cheh)* sample **lista** to help you prepare for your holiday.

TRATTORIA TRE FONTANE

LA LISTA

ANTIPASTI

Antipasti assortiti (assorted appetizers)	£700
Prosciutto crudo di Parma (raw-cured ham)	700
Insalata russa (cooked vegetables and hard-boiled eggs, mixed with mayonnaise)	600
Insalata di pesce (seafood salad)	850

MINESTRE E PASTA

Tortellini in brodo (stuffed pasta in broth)	450
Zuppa di vongole (clam chowder)	350
Zuppa pavese (egg soup)	400
Lasagne a forno (meat, cheese and pasta casserole)	450
Ravioli alla romagnola (pasta stuffed with cheeses)	400
Spaghetti di carne (pasta covered in meat sauce)	350

PESCE

Fritto misto di mare (floured and deep-fried seafood)	1000
Calamaretti fritti (breaded and deep-fried gray mullet)	1000
Sogliola alla Margherita (poached sole covered with Hollandaise sauce)	1500
Cozze alla livornese (mussels in tomato sauce on toast)	850
Spiedino mare (broiled pieces of marinated seafood)	1200

PIATTI DEL GIORNO

Costoletta alla milanese (breaded, unboned veal steak)	850
Abbacchio alla romana (roasted milk-fed lamb)	1200
Vitello tonnato (cold veal cutlets covered in sauce)	1350
Bistecca alla fiorentina (broiled unboned rib steak)	1450
Saltimbocca alla romana (fried slices of veal and ham)	1600

Pollo alla cacciatore (chicken braised in onions, herbs and wine)	1000
Trippe alla bolognese (broiled beef tripe)	800

CONTORNI

Asparagi alla parmigiana (boiled asparagus with Parmesan)	300
Patate fritte (French-fried potatoes)	300
Insalata mista (mixed salad)	300
Insalata verde (green salad)	300
Zucchini trifolati (zucchini cooked in butter and garlic)	400

FORMAGGI

Assortiti a porzione (assorted cheeses)	500

DOLCI

Frutta di stagione, un pezzo (seasonal fruit)	300
St. Honoré (custard pastry and cream puffs dipped in syrup)	500
Cassata alla siciliana (sponge cake layered with sweetened Ricotta cheese, chocolate and fruit)	450
Macedonia di frutta (fruit salad)	450

BEVANDE

Vino (bicchiere)	300
Vino (litro)	1300
Birra	300
Acqua minerale (mineral water)	100
Limonata	150
Succo di frutta (fruit juice)	250
Latte	200
Caffè	150
Tè	150

☐ **vigoroso** *(vee-goh-roh-soh)* .... vigorous

☐ **il vino** *(vee-noh)* .... wine

☐ **la visita** *(vee-see-tah)* .... visit

— **fare una vista** .... to pay a visit

82 ☐ **la vitamina** *(vee-tah-mee-nah)* .... vitamin

La prima colazione *(koh-lah-tsee-oh-neh)* **è un poco differente** because it is fairly standardized **e Lei** will frequently take it at **il Suo albergo** as **è generalmente** included in **il prezzo della Sua camera. Sotto c'è** a sample of what **Lei può** expect to greet you **la mattina.** *(maht-tee-nah)*
in the morning

Colazione 1 . . . . £800

caffelatte
coffee and steamed milk
pane

Colazione 2 . . . . £1,200
(koh-lah-tsee-oh-neh)

caffelatte
(pah-nee-noh)
pane o panino
roll
burro e marmellata
butter   jam

Colazione all'americana
in the American manner

(these additions usually only available in large hotels catering to foreigners)

succo di arancia
orange juice
succo di pompelmo
grapefruit
prosciutto
ham
salsiccia
sausage

uova affogate
egg   poached
uova fritte
fried
uova strapazzate
scrambled
frittata
omelette

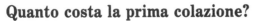

Frasi pratiche

Quanto costa la prima colazione?

Vorrei due caffelatte, per piacere.

(pah-nee-nee)
Vorrei dei panini   e del tè, per favore.
rolls

(vohr-rehb-beh) (fahr) (mohn-tah-reh)
Vorrebbe far montare la prima colazione alla camera
please   have   brought up

dieci, per favore.

_____
_____
_____
_____
_____

Step 19

Che è differente about **il telefono in Italia?** Well, **Lei** never notice such things until **Lei**

want to use them. Be warned **adesso** that **telefoni in Italia** are less numerous than **in**

America. Nevertheless, **il telefono** allows you to reserve **le camere d'albergo in** another

(cheet-tah) *(ah-mee-chee)* *(bahl-let-toh)*
città, call **amici,** reserve **i biglietti di teatro, di concerto o di balletto,** make emergency
city friends ballet

(moo-seh-oh)
calls, check on the hours of a **museo,** rent **una macchina e** all those other **cose** which
museum

(lee-behr-tah)
facciamo on a daily basis. It also gives you a certain amount of **libertà quando Lei può**

(teh-leh-foh-nah-teh)
make your own **telefonate.**
calls

You may not always have **un telefono** in your **albergo in Italia.** This means that **Lei**

(deh-veh) *(seep)*
deve sapere dove trovare i telefoni: in the **ufficio dei telefoni (S.I.P.),** on the **strada,**
must to find

in the **bar,** at the **stazione dei treni** and in the lobby of **il Suo albergo.** Often **Lei deve**

(jet-toh-nee) *(poob-blee-kah)*
comprare a token, called <u>**un gettone,**</u> to use when **Lei fa una telefonata pubblica.**
make

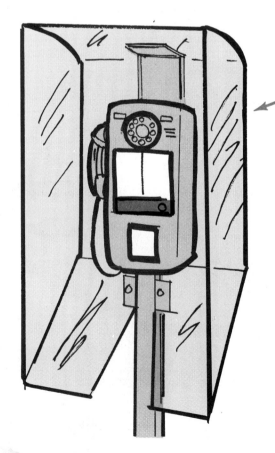

(poob-blee-koh)
Ecco un telefono pubblico italiano.

So far, so good. **Adesso,** let's read the instructions for using **il telefono.** This is one of those moments when you realize,

Non sono in America.

So let's learn how to operate **il telefono.**

If **Lei** use **il telefono in un bar,** be sure to ask, "**È necessario un gettone?**" *(neh-chehs-sah-ree-oh) (jet-toh-neh)* The **bar** employee will sell you **un gettone** to use if it is needed **e,** if not, then **Lei può** use regular **monete.**

TELEFONATA LOCALE:

Inserire il gettone o le monete nella fessura. Alzare il ricevitore e formare
insert   opening   lift   receiver   dial

il numero.

Aspettare la risposta e premere il pulsante che fa scendere il gettone.
wait   answer   press   push button   makes fall

NEL CASO DI UNA TELEFONATA INTERURBANA:
long-distance

Bisogna inserire almeno sei gettoni o £600.
it's necessary   at least

Se la conversazione oltrepassa i tre minuti, bisogna inserire altri gettoni o monete.
goes beyond   other

Alla fine della conversazione interurbana, i gettoni non usati verranno
at the   end   unused   will be

restituiti premendo il pulsante appropriato di restituzione.
returned   pressing   return

Inglese	Italiano	Inglese	Italiano
telephone	= **il telefono**	to telephone	= **telefonare** *(teh-leh-foh-nah-reh)*
			= **fare una telefonata**
telephone booth	= **la cabina telefonica**	operator	= **l'operatore** *(loh-peh-rah-toh-reh)*
telephone book	= **l'elenco telefonico** *(leh-len-koh)*		= **la centralinista** *(chen-trah-lee-nee-stah)*
telephone conversation	= **la conversazione telefonica**	token	= **il gettone**

85

So **adesso Lei sa come fare una telefonata in Italia.** **Lei** will find that **la maggioranza** *(mah-joh-rahn-tsah)*
majority

dei numeri in Italia sono sette digits, such as **522-4500.** **Ci sono anche** area codes,

or **i numeri prefissi,** *(noo-meh-ree)(preh-fees-see)* and these are listed in **l'elenco telefonico.** *(leh-len-koh)* *(teh-leh-foh-nee-koh)*
telephone book

When answering **il telefono, Lei** pick up **il ricevitore e** say: *(ree-cheh-vee-toh-reh)*
receiver

"**Pronto! Sono** _____." *(prohn-toh)*

il Suo nome

When saying good-bye, **Lei dice,** "**A domani**" **o** "**arrivederci.**" **Ecco** some sample *(doh-mah-nee)*
until tomorrow   good-bye

conversazioni al telefono. Write them in the blanks **sotto.**
on the

Vorrei telefonare all'Opera. _____ *(voh-reh-ee)*
I would like

Vorrei telefonare a Chicago. *Vorrei telefonare a Chicago.*

Vorrei telefonare alla signora Sordini a Ostia. _____

Vorrei telefonare al signor Sordini a San Remo. _____

Vorrei telefonare a Alitalia all'aeroporto. _____

Vorrei fare una telefonata "collect." _____

Dov'è la cabina telefonica? _____

Dov'è l'elenco telefonico. _____

Il mio numero è 387-9106. _____

Qual'è il Suo numero di telefono? _____ *(kwah-leh)*
what

Qual'è il numero di telefono dell'albergo? _____

Ecco un'altra conversazione possibile. Listen to **le parole e come** they are used. *(oo-nahl-trah)* *(pohs-see-bee-leh)*
another

Thomas: **Pronto! Sono il signor Martini al telefono. Vorrei parlare alla signora Soleri.**

Segretaria: **Un momento, per favore. Mi scusi, ma la linea è occupata.**
but

Thomas: **Ripeta, per piacere. Parlo solamente un poco d'italiano. Parli più**
(pee-oo)
more
(len-tah-men-teh)
lentamente.
slowly

Segretaria: **Mi scusi, ma la linea è occupata.**

Thomas: **Beh. Grazie. Arrivederci, signorina.**
well

(pohs-see-bee-lee-tah)
Ed ancora un'altra possibilità.

Eva: **Vorrei delle informazioni per Assisi, per favore. Vorrei il numero di telefono del dottor Andrea Rossi, per piacere.**

Operatore: **Il numero è 816-4506.**

Eva: **Ripeta il numero, per favore.**

Operatore: **Il numero è 816-4506.**

Eva: **Molte grazie. Arrivederci.**

Operatore: **Prego. Arrivederci.**
you're welcome

Lei è adesso ready to use any **telefono in Italia.** Just take it **lentamente e** speak clearly.

(dee-men-tee-kee)
Non dimentichi that **Lei può** ask . . .
don't forget

(loh-kah-leh)
Quanto costa una telefonata locale? *Quanto costa una telefonata locale?*
call

(een-tair-oor-bah-nah)
Quanto costa una telefonata interurbana? _____
long-distance

(ahl-yee) (stah-tee) (oo-nee-tee)
Quanto costa una telefonata agli Stati Uniti? _____
to the United States

Quanto costa una telefonata interurbana a Firenze? _____

Non dimentichi that **Lei ha bisogno di monete o di gettoni per il telefono.**
need

87

Step 20

(meh-troh-poh-lee-tah-nah)
La metropolitana, commonly called **"la metro,"** **è il nome per** the subway. *(meh-troh)* **La metro a**

Roma è a quick and cheap form of *(trah-spohr-toh)* **trasporto,** though not as extensive as the *(see-steh-mah)* **sistema**
transportation

di autobus. The route **la metro** follows goes well outside the city limits into the

(sohb-bohr-gee)
sobborghi di Roma. A Roma, e nelle smaller *(cheet-tah)* **città, c'è** *(sem-preh)* **sempre l'autobus,** a slower but
suburbs   cities   always

much more scenic means of *(trah-spohr-toh)* **trasporto. Lei** may also wish to go by **tassì.** In that case,

find a taxi station, hail a **tassì** on the street or have one called **al Suo albergo.** *(kwah-lee)* **Quali**
what

parole sono necessarie per viaggiare in metro, in autobus o in tassì? Let's learn them

by practicing them aloud **e poi** by writing them in the blanks **sotto.**

(meh-troh)
la metro

(tahs-see)
il tassì

(lah-oo-toh-boos)
l'autobus

_____   *il tassì*   _____

la *(fehr-mah-tah)* **fermata** = the stop _____

la *(lee-neh-ah)* **linea** = the line _____

il *(kohn-doot-toh-reh)* **conduttore** = the driver ___*il conduttore*_____

il *(kohn-trohl-loh-reh)* **controllore** = the ticket-collector _____

Let's also review **i verbi di trasporto** at this point.

(sah-lee-reh)
salire = to board/to get into _____

(shehn-deh-reh)
scendere = to get off/to go down ___*scendere*_____

(kahm-bee-ah-reh)
cambiare (autobus) = to transfer (bus) _____

(vee-ah-jah-reh)
88 **viaggiare** = to travel _____

Maps displaying the various **linee e fermate** *(lee-neh) (fehr-mah-teh)* **sono generalmente** posted outside every

entrata *(en-trah-tah)* **della stazione** *(stah-tsee-oh-neh)* **della metro.** Almost every **pianta** *(pee-ahn-tah)* **di Roma** also has a **metro** map included.
map

To **comprare un biglietto, Lei** must put **monete** in a vending machine and the **biglietto**

will come out. **Lei** take **il biglietto** and put it in the slot by the turnstile. When **Lei**

cross through, **il biglietto** comes out. **Lei può** then **salire sul treno.** Check **il nome** of

the **fermata** on the **linea** which you should take **e** catch **il treno** traveling in that

direzione. *(dee-reh-tsee-oh-neh)* If **Lei deve cambiare treno** or transfer to an **autobus,** look for **le coincidenze** *(koh-een-chee-den-tseh)*
connections

clearly marked at each **fermata.** **Il sistema di autobus** works similarly. See **la pianta sotto.** *(pee-ahn-tah)*
map

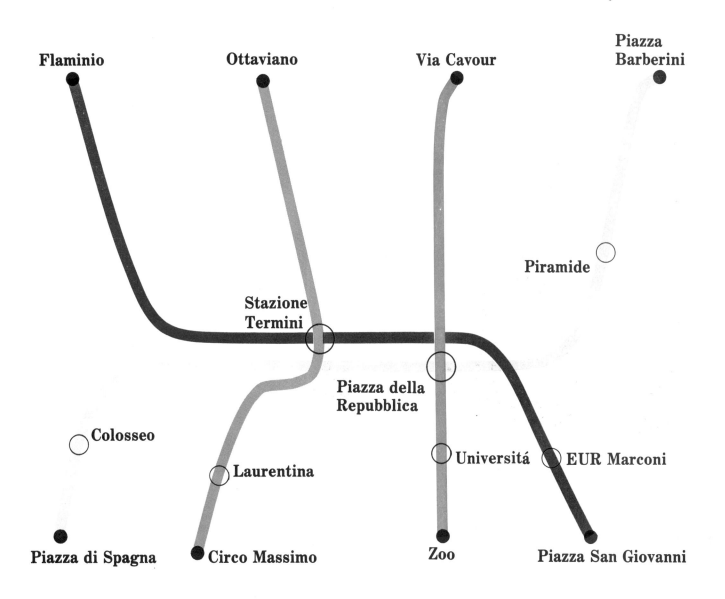

The same basic set of **parole e domande** will see you through traveling **in metro, in autobus,**

in macchina o even **in treno.**

Naturally, la (pree-mah) **prima domanda** è "dove."

> Dov'è la (fehr-mah-tah) **fermata** della (meh-troh) **metro**?
>
> Dov'è la **fermata** dell'autobus?
>
> Dov'è il (poh-steh-joh) **posteggio** dei tassì?
> parking place

Practice the following basic **domande** out loud **e poi** write them in the blanks **a destra**.

1. **Dov'è la fermata della metro?** _____

   Dov'è la fermata dell'autobus? *Dov'è la fermata dell'autobus?*

   (poh-steh-joh)
   Dov'è il posteggio dei tassì? _____

2. **Qual'è la (freh-kwen-tsah) frequenza dei treni per il Colosseo?** _____
   frequency

   Qual'è la frequenza degli autobus per il (vah-tee-kah-noh) Vaticano? _____

   Qual'è la frequenza dei tassì per l'aeroporto? _____

3. (kwahn-doh) **Quando parte il treno?** _____
   when

   Quando parte l'autobus? _____

   Quando parte il tassì? _____

4. **Quando parte il treno per (tee-voh-lee) Tivoli?** _____

   Quando parte l'autobus per (pah-ree-oh-lee) Parioli? _____

   Quando parte il tassì per l'aeroporto? _____

5. **Quanto costa un biglietto della metro?** _____

   Quanto costa un biglietto dell'autobus? _____

   Quanto è la (tah-reef-fah) tariffa? *Quanto è la tariffa?*
   fare

   Quanto le (deh-voh) devo? _____
   to you I owe

Adesso that **Lei ha** gotten into the swing of things, practice the following patterns aloud,

substituting "**autobus**" for "**metro**" **e** so on.

1. **Dove si compra un biglietto della metro? dell'autobus? del treno?**

2. **Quando parte il treno per il Foro Romano? per il centro della città?** *(chen-troh)* *(cheet-tah)* **per il Colosseo?**

   per la Stazione Termini? per il Circo Massimo? *(cheer-koh)(mahs-see-moh)*

3. **Dov'è la fermata della metro per andare al Piramide?** *(pee-rah-mee-deh)*

   Dov'è la fermata dell'autobus per andare al Foro Italico?

   Dov'è la fermata della metro per andare al centro della città?

   Dov'è la fermata dell'autobus per andare allo zoo? *(zoh)*

   Dov'è la fermata della metro per andare al Museo di *(ahr-teh)* *(moh-dair-nah)* **Arte Moderna?**

   Dov'è la fermata dell'autobus per andare a Piazza Venezia?

   Dov'è la fermata della metro per andare a Cinecittà? *(chee-neh-cheet-tah)*

   Dov'è la fermata dell'autobus per andare a Piazza Navona? *(nah-voh-nah)*

PIAZZA >
< COLOSSEO
PIRAMIDE >
< CIRCO MASSIMO
ZOO >
< UNIVERSITÀ

(lehg-gah)
Legga la conversazione seguente, molto tipica, **e la scriva** in the blanks **a destra**.
read   it

Qual'è la linea a Piazza Barberini? *(bahr-beh-ree-nee)* _____
which

La linea gialla va a Piazza Barberini. _____

Con che frequenza? _____

(ohn-yee)
Ogni cinque minuti. _____ *Ogni cinque minuti.*
every
(deh-voh)
Devo cambiare treno? _____

Sí, alla Stazione Termini. Lei ha una coincidenza alla Stazione Termini. *(koh-een-chee-den-zah)*
                                                    connection

Sí, alla Stazione Termini. _____

Quanti minuti ci vogliono per andare da qui a Cinecittà? *(chee)* *(vohl-yoh-noh)* *(kwee)* *(chee-neh-cheet-tah)* _____
                  it   takes   from here

(vohl-yoh-noh)
Ci vogliono 20 minuti. _____
it   takes

Quanto costa il biglietto per Cinecittà? _____

Due cento lire. _____ 91

Può Lei translate the following thoughts **in italiano?** **Le risposte sono sotto.**

1. Where is the subway stop? _____

2. What costs a ticket to Piazza Navona? _____

3. How often do the buses go to the airport? _____

4. Where does one buy a subway ticket?_____

5. Where is the bus stop? *Dov'è la fermata dell'autobus?*

6. I would like to get out. _____

7. Must I transfer?_____

8. Where must I transfer?_____

Ecco ancora tre verbi.

(lah-vah-reh)
lavare = to wash

(pehr-deh-reh)
perdere = to lose

(chee)(voo-oh-leh)
ci vuole
(chee)(vohl-yoh-noh) = it takes
ci vogliono

lavare _____ _____ _____

Lei know the basic "plug-in" formula, so translate the following thoughts **con questi nuovi verbi.** **Le risposte sono anche sotto.**

1. I wash the car. _____

2. You lose the book. _____

3. It takes 20 minutes to go to Parma. _____

4. It takes three hours by car. _____

(vehn-deh-reh)   *(kohm-prah-reh)*

Il Vendere e il Comprare

selling   buying

Shopping abroad **è** exciting. The simple everyday task of buying **un litro di latte o una**

(meh-lah)
mela becomes a challenge that **Lei** should **adesso** be able to meet quickly **e** easily. Of
apple

course, **Lei** will purchase **dei ricordi, dei francobolli, e delle cartoline**, but **non**
(ree-kohr-dee)
souvenirs

(dee-men-tee-kee)   *(ah-spee-ree-nah)*
dimentichi those many other **cose** ranging from shoelaces to **aspirina** that **Lei** might
forget   aspirin

(sah)   *(lee-breh-ree-ah)*   *(mah-chehl-leh-ree-ah)*
need unexpectedly. **Sa Lei la differenza fra una libreria e una macelleria?** No.
know   bookstore   butcher shop

(neh-goh-tsee)   *(boht-teh-geh)*   *(cheh)*   *(pee-ahn-tah)*
Let's learn about the different **negozi e botteghe in Italia. Sotto c'è una pianta di**
stores   shops   map

(seh-tsee-oh-neh)
una sezione di Roma.
section

Alle pagine seguenti, ci sono all types of **negozi in Italia.** Be sure to fill in the blanks **sotto**
(neh-goh-tsee)

le illustrazioni con il nome del negozio.
of the

il panificio, *(pah-nee-fee-choh)*
bakery

dove si compra il pane *(see)*
one buys

la macelleria, *(mah-chel-leh-ree-ah)*
butcher shop

dove si compra la carne *(see)* *(kahr-neh)*
one

la lavanderia, *(lah-vahn-deh-ree-ah)*
laundry

dove si lavano i vestiti *(veh-stee-tee)*
washes

la macelleria

il bar, *(bahr)*

dove si beve il caffè *(beh-veh)*
drinks

o il vino o il whisky

la ferramenta, *(fehr-rah-men-tah)*
hardware store

dove si compra la pila *(pee-lah)*
battery

la farmacia, *(fahr-mah-chee-ah)*
pharmacy

dove si compra l'aspirina *(lah-spee-ree-nah)*

il bar

il fioraio, *(fee-oh-rah-ee-oh)*
florist

dove si comprano i fiori

sali e tabacchi, dove si *(sah-lee) (tah-bahk-kee)*
salt   tobacco

compra il sale o

il tabacco

la confetteria, *(kohn-fet-teh-ree-ah)*
candy store

dove si compra

il cioccolato *(chok-koh-lah-toh)*

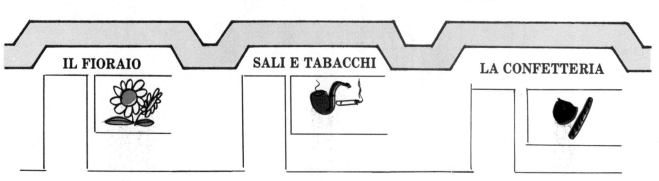

la latteria, *(laht-teh-ree-ah)*
dairy

dove si compra il latte

la pasticceria, *(pah-stee-cheh-ree-ah)*
pastry shop

dove si comprano i dolci *(dohl-chee)*
sweets/pastries

l'erbivendolo, *(lehr-bee-ven-doh-loh)*
greengrocer

dove si comprano le verdure *(vehr-doo-reh)*
vegetables

LA LATTERIA | LA PASTICCERIA | L'ERBIVENDOLO

il parcheggio, *(pahr-keh-joh)*
parking lot

dove si parcheggia la *(pahr-keh-jah)*
park

macchina

il parrucchiere, *(pahr-rook-kee-eh-reh)*
hairdresser

dove si tagliano i *(tahl-yah-noh)*
cut

capelli *(kah-pel-lee)*
hair

il sarto/la sarta, *(sahr-toh)* *(sahr-tah)*
tailor /seamstress

dove si fanno i vestiti *(fahn-noh)* *(veh-stee-tee)*
make

IL PARRUCCHIERE | IL SARTO/LA SARTA

il sarto/la sarta

l'ufficio postale,
post office

dove si comprano i

francobolli

la questura, *(kweh-stoo-rah)*
police station

dove si trova la polizia *(poh-lee-tsee-ah)*
police

la banca, *(bahn-kah)*
bank

dove si cambia
exchanges/cashes

il denaro

L'UFFICIO POSTALE | LA QUESTURA | LA BANCA

95

(soo-pehr-mehr-kah-toh)
il supermercato,
grocery store

dove si compra la carne o

la frutta o il latte

(sah-loo-meh-ree-ah)
la salumeria,
delicatessen

(sah-loo-mee)
dove si comprano i salumi
sausages/salami

(froot-tee-ven-doh-loh)
il fruttivendolo,
fruit seller

(froot-tah)
dove si compra la frutta
fruit

IL SUPERMERCATO

LA SALUMERIA

IL FRUTTIVENDOLO

(chee-neh-mah)
il cinema,
movie house

(veh-deh) **(feelm)**
dove si vede il film
sees

(johr-nah-lah-ee-oh)
il giornalaio,
newsstand

(johr-nah-lee)
dove si comprano i giornali

(ree-vee-steh)
e le riviste

(teen-toh-ree-ah)
la tintoria,
dry cleaner's

(lah-vah-joh)
dove si fa il lavaggio a
cleaning

(sehk-koh)
secco
dry

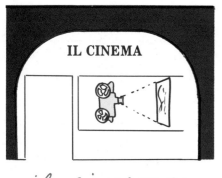

IL CINEMA

IL GIORNALAIO

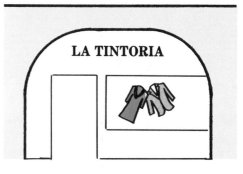

LA TINTORIA

il cinema

(kahr-toh-leh-ree-ah)
la cartoleria,
stationery store

dove si compra la carta,

o la penna o la matita

(lee-breh-ree-ah)
la libreria,
bookstore

dove si comprano e si

vendono i libri

(mah-gah-tsee-noh)
il grande magazzino,
department store

(toot-toh)
dove si compra tutto
everything

(see Step 22)

LA CARTOLERIA

LA LIBRERIA

IL GRANDE MAGAZZINO

(mehr-kah-toh)
il mercato, dove si comprano
market

le verdure e la frutta

(lee-pehr-mehr-kah-toh)
l'ipermercato
supermarket

dove si compra tutto
everything

(stah-tsee-on-neh)
la stazione di benzina,
gas station

dove si compra la benzina

l'ipermercato

(lah-jehn-tsee-ah) *(vee-ah-jee)*
l'agenzia di viaggi,
travel agency

dove si compra un

biglietto dell'aeroplano

(loh-roh-loh-jeh-ree-ah)
l'orologeria,
clock and watchmaker's shop

dove si comprano gli

orologi

(pen-sken-ree-ah)
la pescheria,
fish market

dove si compra il pesce *(peh-sheh)*
fish

Quando sono *(ah-pehr-tee)* **aperti i** *(neh-goh-tsee)* **negozi italiani? I negozi italiani sono generalmente aperti da**
are   open   stores

lunedì a sabato, dalle 9,00 alle 18,30. Molti negozi will close over the lunch hour

(12,00 — 14,00). Many shops **sono anche** closed **il lunedì.** Local, open-air **mercati**

sono truly **un'esperienza,** *(oo-neh-speh-ree-en-zah)* so be sure to check **le** *(leh)* **ore** *(oh-reh)* of the one closest to **il Suo**
experience   hours

albergo.

C'è anything else which makes **i negozi italiani differenti** from **i negozi americani? Sí.**
is there

Look at **le illustrazioni alla pagina seguente.**

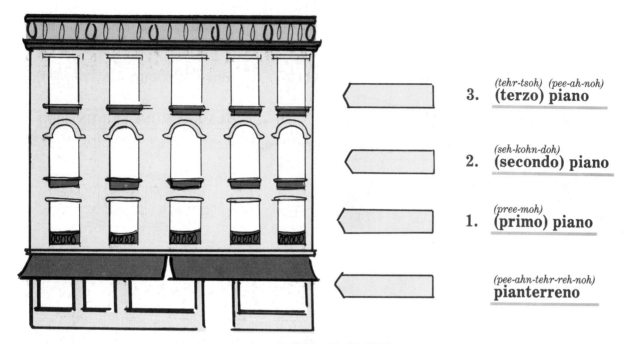

3. *(tehr-tsoh) (pee-ah-noh)*
(terzo) piano

2. *(seh-kohn-doh)*
(secondo) piano

1. *(pree-moh)*
(primo) piano

(pee-ahn-tehr-reh-noh)
pianterreno

In Italia, the ground floor **si chiama "il** *(pee-ahn-tehr-reh-noh)* **pianterreno."** The first floor **è** the next floor up **e** so on. Now that **Lei** know **i nomi dei negozi italiani,** let's practice shopping.

I. First step — **Dove?**

Dov'è la latteria?   **Dov'è la banca?**   **Dov'è il cinema?**

Go through **i negozi** introduced in this Step **e** ask **"Dove"** con *(ohn-yee)* **ogni negozio.** Another way of asking **dove** is to ask

(cheh)   *(kwee) (vee-chee-noh)*
C'è una latteria qui vicino?
is there   here   near   **C'è una banca qui vicino?**

Go through **i negozi** again using *(kwehs-tah)* **questa nuova domanda.**
this

II. Next step — tell them what **Lei** are looking for, need **o vorrebbe!**

1) *(oh) (bee-sohn-yoh)* **Ho bisogno di . . .** *Ho bisogno di* _____

2) **Ha Lei . . . ?** _____

3) **Vorrei . . .** _____

Ho bisogno di una matita.

Ha Lei una matita?

Vorrei una matita.

Ho bisogno di un *(kee-loh)* chilo di *(meh-leh)* mele.

Ha Lei un chilo di mele?

Vorrei un chilo di mele.

Go through the glossary at the end of **questo libro e** select **venti parole.** Drill the above patterns **con questi venti parole.** Don't cheat. Drill them **oggi. Adesso,** take **ancora**

more

venti parole dal Suo glossary **e** do the same.

III. Next step — find out **quanto costa.**

1) **Quanto è?** _____

2) **Quanto costa?** _____

Quanto costa la matita?

Quanto costa una cartolina?

Quanto costa il francobollo?

Quanto costa un chilo di mele?

Quanto costa un chilo di *(ah-rahn-cheh)* arancie?

Quanto costa un chilo di carne?

Using these same **parole** that **Lei** selected **sopra,** drill **anche queste domande.**

IV. If **Lei non sa dove trovare** something, **Lei domanda**

ask

Dove si compra l'aspirina?
(lah-spee-ree-nah)

Dove si comprano gli occhiali da sole?
(ohk-kee-ah-lee) *(soh-leh)*
sunglasses

Once **Lei trova** what **Lei** would like, **Lei dice,**   **Vorrei questo, per favore.**

O, if **Lei** would not like it,   **Non vorrei questo, grazie.**

Adesso Lei è all set to shop for anything!

Step 22

(grahn-deh)   *(mah-gah-tsee-noh)*

Il Grande Magazzino
department store

At this point, **Lei** should just about be ready for **il Suo viaggio in Italia. Lei** have gone

shopping for those last-minute odds 'n ends. Most likely, the store directory at your local

(mah-gah-tsee-noh)

grande magazzino did not look like the one **sotto. Lei** already know **molte parole e Lei**

(ahl-treh)   *(bahm-bee-noh)*   *(seen-yee-fee-kah)*

può guess at **molte altre. Lei sa che "bambino" significa** "child," so if **Lei ha**
others   means

bisogno di something **per un bambino, Lei** would probably look on the **secondo o terzo**

piano, vero?

6. PIANO	alimentari tavola calda salumeria	pollame frutta verdure prodotti surgelati	vino cacciagione carne
5. PIANO	letti lenzuoli specchi	mobili lampade tappeti	quadri elettrodomestici
4. PIANO	cristalleria vasellame da cucina	servizi da tavola mobili da cucina	chiavi ceramici porcellana
3. PIANO	libri televisori mobili da bambini giocattoli	radio strumenti musicali cartoleria dischi	ristorante giornali riviste
2. PIANO	tutto per il bambino vestiti da donna cappelli da donna	vestiti da uomo scarpe da bambino foto	gabinetti antiquario
1. PIANO	accessori da macchina fazzoletti biancheria	costumi da bagno scarpe da donna scarpe da uomo	articoli sportivi articoli da campeggio ferramenta
P	ombrelli biglietti di auguri cappelli da uomo gioielleria	guanti articoli di pelle e cuoio calze	cinture orologi profumeria pasticceria

(veh-stee-tee)   *(keh)*   *(bee-sohn-yoh)*

Let's start a checklist **per il Suo viaggio.** Besides **vestiti, di che ha bisogno Lei?**
clothing

100 Che è necessario in Europa?

(pahs-sah-pohr-toh)
il **passaporto**

(beel-yet-toh)
il **biglietto**

(vah-lee-jah)
la **valigia**

la valigia ✓

(bohr-sah)
la **borsa**

(pohr-tah-fohl-yoh)
il **portafoglio**

(deh-nah-roh)
il **denaro**

(mahk-kee-nah) *(foh-toh-grah-fee-kah)*
la **macchina fotografica** →

(pel-lee-koh-lah)
la **pellicola**

(prehn-dah)
Prenda gli otto prossimi labels **e** label **queste cose oggi.** Better yet, assemble them **in un**
take

angolo della Sua casa.

Viaggia Lei in Italia in estate o in inverno? Non *(dee-men-tee-kee)* **dimentichi...**
don't forget

(koh-stoo-mee) *(bahn-yoh)*
i **costumi da bagno**

(sahn-dah-lee)
i **sandali**

Non dimentichi *(neh-ahn-keh)* **neanche** the basic toiletries!
either

(sah-poh-neh)
il **sapone**

il sapone ✓

(spah-tsoh-lee-noh) *(den-tee)*
lo **spazzolino da denti**

(den-tee-free-choh)
il **dentifricio**

(rah-soh-ee-oh)
il **rasoio**

(deh-oh-doh-rahn-teh)
il **deodorante**

(pet-tee-neh)
il **pettine**

101

For the rest of the **cose,** let's start **con** the outside layers **e** work our way in.

(soh-prah-bee-toh)
il soprabito _____ ✓

(leem-pehr-meh-ah-bee-leh)
l'impermeabile _____ ☐

(lohm-brel-loh)
l'ombrello _____ ☐

(gwahn-tee)
i guanti _____ ☐

(kahp-pel-loh)
il cappello _____ ☐

(stee-vah-leh)
lo stivale _____*lo stivale*_____ ☐

(skahr-pah)
la scarpa _____ ☐

(kahl-tsee-noh)
il calzino _____ ✓

(kahl-tseh)
le calze _____ ☐

(prehn-dah)
Prenda i quindici prossimi labels **e** label **queste cose.** Check **e** make sure that **sono puliti**
take   *(poo-lee-tee)*
                                                                          clean

e ready **per il Suo viaggio.** Check them off on **questa lista** as **Lei** organize them. From

now on, **Lei ha il** *(den-tee-free-choh)* **"dentifricio" e non il** "toothpaste."

(pee-jah-mah)
il pigiama _____*il pigiama*_____ ☐

(kah-mee-chet-tah) *(noht-teh)*
la camicetta da notte _____ ☐

(lahk-kahp-pah-toh-ee-oh)
L'accappatoio _____ ☐
bathrobe

(pahn-toh-foh-leh)
le pantofole _____ ☐

(lahk-kahp-pah-toh-ee-oh)   *(pohs-soh-noh)*   *(spee-ah-jah)*
102 **L'accappatoio e le pantofole possono anche** double **per Lei alla spiaggia.**
   bathrobe   slippers   can   beach

(lah-bee-toh)
l'abito _____ ☐

(krah-vaht-tah)
la cravatta _____ ☐

(fah-tsoh-let-toh)
il fazzoletto _____ ☐

(kah-mee-chah)
la camicia _____ ☐

(jahk-kah)
la giacca _____ ☐

(pahn-tah-loh-nee)
i pantaloni _____ ✓

(veh-stee-toh)
il vestito _____ ☐

(kah-mee-chet-tah)
la camicetta _la camicetta_ ☐

(gohn-nah)
la gonna _____ ☐

(mahl-yah)
la maglia _____ ☐

(reh-jee-pet-toh)
il reggipetto _____ ☐

(soht-toh-veh-steh)
la sottoveste _____ ☐

(moo-tahn-deh)
le mutande _____ ☐

(kah-noht-tee-eh-rah)
la canottiera _____ ☐

(prohn-toh)
Having assembled **queste cose, Lei è pronto per il Suo viaggio.** However, being human
_{these} _{ready}

means occasionally forgetting something. Look again at **il grande magazzino** directory.

A quale piano Lei trova . . .
_{floor}

(oo-oh-moh)
vestiti da uomo?   Al ___2___ **piano.**
_{man}

un cappello per una donna?   Al _____ **piano.**

libri?   Al _____ **piano.**

(bee-ahn-keh-ree-ah)
biancheria?   Al _____ **piano.**
_{lingerie}

103

(kree-stahl-lair-ee-ah)
cristalleria?   Al _____ **piano.**

(proh-foo-mair-ee-ah)
profumeria?   Al _____ .

vestiti da donna?   Al _____ **piano.**

Adesso, just remember your basic **domande.** **Ripeta la conversazione tipica sotto**

out loud **e poi** by filling in the blanks.

Dove si trovano i pantaloni da donna? _____

(reh-pahr-toh)
Nel reparto dei vestiti da donna. _____
_{department}

Dov'è il reparto dei vestiti da donna? _____

Al secondo piano. _____ *Al secondo piano.* _____

Dove si trovano il sapone ed il dentifricio? _____

Al pianterreno. _____

Anche, non dimentichi di *(doh-mahn-dah-reh)* **domandare . . .**
_{to ask}

(lah-shen-soh-reh)
Dov'è l'ascensore? _____
_{elevator}

(skah-leh)
Dove sono le scale? _____
_{stairs}

(moh-bee-leh)
Dov'è la scala mobile? _____
_{escalator}

Whether **Lei ha bisogno di pantaloni da donna o di una camicia da** *(oo-oh-moh)* **uomo, le parole**

necessarie sono the same. Practice your **nuove parole con i vestiti seguenti. Dov'è la**

gonna? Dov'è...

Che *(tahl-yah)* **taglia?**
size

_____

Che *(mee-soo-rah)* **misura?**
size for shoes and gloves

_____

Questo *(mee)* **mi** *(vah)* **va.**
me   fits

Questo mi va.

Questo non mi va.

_____

(prehn-doh)
Prendo questo.
I take   this

_____

Quanto è?

_____

È *(toot-toh)* **tutto, grazie.**
that's   all

_____

Clothing sizes: **DONNE** *(dohn-neh)*
women

scarpe									
American	5	5½	6	6½	7	7½	8	8½	9
Continental	35	35	36	37	38	38	38	39	40

vestiti						
American	8	10	12	14	16	18
Continental	36	38	40	42	44	46

camicette, maglie						
American	32	34	36	38	40	42	44
Continental	40	42	44	46	48	50	52

Clothing sizes: **UOMINI** *(oo-oh-mee-nee)*
men

scarpe										
American	7	7½	8	8½	9	9½	10	10½	11	11½
Continental	39	40	41	42	43	43	44	44	45	45

vestiti								
American	34	36	38	40	42	44	46	48
Continental	44	46	48	50	52	54	56	58

camicie								
American	14	14½	15	15½	16	16½	17	17½
Continental	36	37	38	39	40	41	42	43

Adesso, Lei è pronto per il Suo viaggio. Lei sa tutto that you need. The next Step will give you a quick review of international road signs **e** then **Lei** are off to **l'aeroporto.**

Buon viaggio! Buon divertimento!

Step 23

 = Dangerous Intersection

Ecco some of the most important **segnali stradali** *(sen-yah-lee) (strah-dah-lee)* signs road **internazionali.** *(een-tehr-nah-tsee-oh-nah-lee)* international Remember that **in**

Italia a basic rule of the road is **priorità a   destra.** *(pree-oh-ree-tah)* yield to the right **Guidi attentamente!** *(gwee-dee)(aht-ten-tah-men-teh)* drive carefully **Buon viaggio!**

Danger

Dangerous
curve

Dangerous
intersection

Closed to
all vehicles

Prohibited for
motor vehicles

Prohibited for
motor vehicles
on Sundays and
holidays

No entry

Stop

Main road ahead,
yield the right
of way

You have the
right of way

Additional
sign indicating
the right of way

One-way street

Dead-end street

Detour

Traffic circle

| No left turn | No U-turn | No parking | No parking or waiting |

| No passing | Speed limit | End of speed limit | Beginning of **autostrada** |

| Railroad crossing 240 meters | Railroad crossing 160 meters | Railroad crossing 80 meters | Customs |

| Federal Highway Number | End of city limit | Parking permitted | Road ends, water ahead |

GLOSSARY

A

a .... at, to
a domani .... until tomorrow
abbiamo/avere .... we have/to have
abitare .... to live, to reside
abito, l' .... suit
accanto a .... next to
accappatoio, l' .... bathrobe
accelerato, l' .... slow train
acqua, l' .... water
adesso .... now
aereo, l'; aereoplano, l' .... airplane
aereoporto, l' .... airport
agenzia di noleggio, l' . car rental agency
agenzia di viaggi, l' .... travel agency
agli .... to the
agnello, l' .... lamb
agosto .... August
al forno .... baked
albergatore, l' .... hotelkeeper
albergo, l' .... hotel
alcool, l' .... alcohol
alcune, alcuni .... some
alfabeto, l' .... alphabet
alla griglia .... grilled
al, alla, alle, allo .... to the, at the
almeno .... at least
alte, alto .... high
altre, altro .... others
alzare .... to lift
America, l' .... America
americano, l' .... American
amica, l'; amico, l' (gli amici) .... friend
anche, anch' .... also
ancora .... more, still
andare .... to go
andata e ritorno .... round-trip
angolo, l' .... corner
anno, l' .... year
antipasti, gli .... appetizers
aperto .... open
appetito, l' .... appetite
appuntamenti, gli .... appointments
apra .... open
aprile .... April
arancia, l' (le arancie) .... orange
aranciata, l' .... orangeade
armadietto di cucina, l' ...... cupboard
armadio, l' .... wardrobe
arriva/arrivare .. arrive, arrives/to arrive
arriverderci .... good-bye
arrivo, l' .... arrival
arrosto .... roasted
ascensore, l' .... elevator
asciugamani, gli .... towels
  asciugamano da bagno, l' .. bath towel
  asciugamano grande, l' .... large towel
  asciugamano piccolo, l' .... hand towel
aspettare .... to wait for
aspirina, l' .... aspirin
attentamente .... carefully
attenzione, l' .... attention
atterrare .... to land
attore, l' .... actor
attraverso .... across
auto, l' .... car
autobus, l' .... bus
autostrada, l' .... highway
autunno, l' .... autumn
avere .... to have
avere bisogno di .... to need
azzurro .... blue

B

bagagli, i .... bags, suitcases
bagnarsi .... to bathe
balleto, il .... ballet
bambino, il (i bambini) .... child
banana, la .... banana
banca, la .... bank
bar, il .... bar, pub
barca, la .... boat
basato .... based
basse .... low
beh .... oh, well
bel, bella, bello .... nice, beautiful
bene .... good
benedizione, la .... benediction
benzina, la .... gas
bere .... to drink
bevande, le .... beverages
biancheria, la .... lingerie
bianco .... white
bicchiere, il (i bicchieri) .... glass
bicicletta, la .... bicycle
biglietto, il (i biglietti) .... bank note, bill, ticket
  biglietti dell'autobus, i .... bus tickets
  biglietti teatrali, i ..... theater tickets
binario, il .... train track
birra, la (le birre) .... beer
bisogno, il .... need
bistecca, la .... steak
bolle .... boils
borsa, la .... handbag, purse
botteghe, le .... stores, shops
bottiglia, la .... bottle
breve .... brief, short
buca delle lettere, la .... mailbox
buon, buona, buono .... good
  buona fortuna .... good luck
  buon giorno .... good morning, good afternoon
  buona notte .... good night
  buona sera .... good evening
  buon viaggio .... have a good trip!
burro, il .... butter

C

cabina telefonica, la ... telephone booth
cacciagione, la .... wild game
caffè, il .... coffee
  caffelatte, il .. coffee and steamed milk
caldo .... warm, hot
calendario, il .... calendar
calze, le .... nylon stockings
calzino, il (i calzini) .... sock
cambiare (treno) ..... to transfer (train)
camera, la .... room
camera da letto, la .... bedroom
cameriera, la .... waitress
cameriere, il .... waiter
camicetta, la .... blouse
camicetta da notte, la .... nightshirt
camicia, la .... shirt
campanello, il .... doorbell
cane, il .... dog
canottiera, la .... undershirt
cantina, la .... cellar
capelli, i .... hair
capire .... to understand
cappello, il .... hat
cappotto, il .... overcoat
cara, caro .... expensive
caramelle, le .... caramels, candies
carne, la .... meat
carta, la .... paper, map
cartoleria, la .... stationery store
cartolina, la .... postcard
casa, la .... house
cassa, la .... cashier's desk
castello, il .... castle
categoria, la .... category
cattedrale, la .... cathedral
cattivo .... bad
cattolica .... Catholic
c'è .... there is
cena, la .... dinner
cento .... one hundred
centralinista, la ..... telephone operator
centro, il .... center, downtown
certo .... certainly
cestino, il .... wastebasket
che .... what
chi .... who
chiama/chiamarsi .. call, calls/to be called
chiesa, la .... church
chili, i .... kilos
chiuso .... closed
ci sono .... there are
ci vogliono, ci vuole .... it takes
ciao .... hi!/bye!
cinema, il .... cinema, movie house
cinquanta .... fifty
cinque .... five
cioccolato, il .... chocolate
cioccolata, la .... hot chocolate
città, la .... city
coincidenze, le .... train connections
colazione, la .... breakfast, lunch
colore, il (i colori) .... color
coltello, il .... knife
come .... how
comincia .... begin, begins
compra, comprano/comprare .... buy, buys/to buy
comunicazione, la .... communication
con .... with
concerto, il .... concert
conduttore, il .... driver
confetteria, la .... candy store
continui .... continue
conto, il .... bill
contorni, i .... vegetables
contravvenzione, la .... traffic ticket
controllore, il .... ticket-collector
conversazione, la .... conversation
coperta, la .... blanket
corretto .... correct
corridoio, il .... hallway
corta, corto .... short
cose, le .... things
costa/costare .... cost, costs/to cost
costume, il .... custom
cotto .... cooked
cravatta, la .... tie
cucette, le .... berths
cucchiaio, il .... spoon
cucina, la .... kitchen
costume da bagno, il .... bathing suit
cristallo, il .... crystal
cucina, la .... kitchen, stove
cugina, la; cugino, il .... cousin
cuoco, il .... cook
cuscino, il .... pillow

D

da .... of, from
dal, dalla .... from the
davanti a .... in front of
decorato .... decorated
degli, dei, del, delle .... some, of the
denaro, il .... money
delizioso .... delicious
dentrifricio, il .... toothpaste

deodorante, il . . . . deodorant
desidera . . . . desire, desires
desserti, i . . . . desserts
destra . . . . right
  a destra . . . . to the right
deve/dovere
  . . . . . should, owe, owes/to have to, to owe
deviazione, la . . . . detour
di . . . . of, in
di nuovo . . . . again
dicembre . . . . December
diciannove . . . . nineteen
diciassette . . . . seventeen
dieci . . . . ten
diciotto . . . . eighteen
dietro . . . . behind
differente, differenti . . . . different
difficile . . . . difficult
dimentichi . . . . forget
dire . . . . to say
direttissimo, il; diretto, il . . . . . fast train
diretto . . . . direct
direzione, la (le direzioni) . . . . direction
diritto . . . . straight ahead
distanza, la . . . . distance
divertimento, il . . . . fun
dizionario, il . . . . dictionary
dodici . . . . twelve
doccia, la . . . . shower
dogana, la . . . . customs
dolce, il . . . . pastry, sweet
dollaro, il . . . . dollar
domanda, la (le domande) . . . . . question
domani . . . . tomorrow
domenica . . . . Sunday
donna, la (le donne) . . . . woman
dopo . . . . after
dormire . . . . to sleep
dottore, il . . . . doctor
dove . . . . where
  dov'è . . . . where is
  dove sono . . . . where are
dovere . . . . to have to/to owe
dubbio, il . . . . doubt
due . . . . two
durante . . . . during

E

è . . . . is
e . . . . and
e mezzo . . . . half past
e un quarto . . . . a quarter past
ebraica, ebreo . . . . Jewish
eccellente . . . . excellent
ecco . . . . here is, there is
economica . . . . inexpensive
ed . . . . and
elefante, l' . . . . elephant
elenco telefonico, l' . . . . . telephone book
entra/entrare . . . . . enter, enters/to enter
entrata, l' . . . . entrance
  entrata principale, l' . . . main entrance
  entrata laterale, l' . . . . . side entrance
erba, l' . . . . grass
erbivendolo, l' . . . . green grocer
esempio, l' (gli esempi) . . . . . . example
espressioni, le . . . . expressions
espresso, l' . . . . very fast train
est, l' . . . . east
  dell'est . . . . eastern
estate, l' . . . . summer
Europa, l' . . . . Europe

F

FFSS, le . . . . . . Italian national railroad

---

fa/fare . . . .
  . . . . do, does; make, makes/to do, to make
facchino, il . . . . porter
facile . . . . easy
fame, la . . . . hunger
famiglia, la . . . . family
farcito . . . . stuffed
fare . . . . to do, to make
farmacia, la . . . . . pharmacy, drugstore
favore, il . . . . favor
  per favore . . . . please
fazzoletto, il . . . . handkerchief
Febbraio . . . . February
fede, la . . . . faith
fermata, la (le fermate) . . . . stop
ferramenta, la . . . . . hardware store
ferrovia, la (le ferrovie) . . . . . railroad
fessura, la . . . . opening
figli, i . . . . children
figlia, la . . . . daughter
figlio, il . . . . son
film, il . . . . film
finalmente . . . . finally
fine, la . . . . end
finestra, la . . . . window
fioraio, il . . . . florist
fiore, il (i fiori) . . . . flower
fisso . . . . fixed
foglio, il (i fogli) . . . . piece
fontana, la . . . . fountain
forchetta, la . . . . fork
foresta, la . . . . forest
forma, la . . . . form
formaggio, il . . . . cheese
formare . . . . dial (the telephone)
forte . . . . loudly
fortuna, la . . . . luck
fra . . . . between
Francia, la . . . . France
francobollo, il . . . . stamp
frase, la (le frasi) . . . . phrase
fratello . . . . brother
freddo . . . . cold
frequenza, la . . . . frequency
fresco . . . . cool, fresh
frigorifero, il . . . . refrigerator
fritto . . . . fried
frutta, la . . . . fruit
fruttivendolo, il . . . . fruit seller
fumare . . . . to smoke

G

gabinetto, il (i gabinetti) . . . . . . lavatory
garage, il . . . . garage
gatto, il . . . . cat
gela . . . . freezes
generalmente . . . . generally
genitori, i . . . . parents
gennaio . . . . January
gentilezza, la . . . . politeness
gettone, il . . . . token (for telephone calls)
giacca, la . . . . jacket
giallo . . . . yellow
giardino, il . . . . garden
giornalaio, il . . . .
  . . . . newspaper and magazine vendor
giornale, il . . . . newspaper
giorno, il, (i giorni) . . . . day
giovane . . . . young
giovedì . . . . Thursday
giri . . . . turn
giugno . . . . June
gli . . . . the
gondola, la . . . . Venetian boat
gonna, la . . . . skirt
gradi . . . . degrees
grande . . . . grand, big, large
grande magazzino, il . . . department store

---

grazie . . . . thank you
grigio . . . . gray
grosso . . . . thick
guanto, il (i guanti) . . . . glove
guanto da bagno, il . . . . washglove
guardi . . . . look at
guida, la . . . . guide
guidare . . . . to drive

H

ho/avere . . . . I have/to have

I

idea, l' . . . . idea
identiche, identico . . . . identical
ieri . . . . yesterday
illustrazioni, le . . . . pictures
immaginazione, l' . . . . imagination
impari/imparare . . . . . . learn/to learn
impermeabile, l' . . . . raincoat
ipermercato, l' . . . . supermarket
importante . . . . important
in . . . . in, into
indirizzo, l' . . . . address
individuale . . . . . . individual, single
influenza, l' . . . . . influence, influenza
informazione, l' . . . . information
Inghilterra, l' . . . . England
inglese . . . . English
ingresso, l' . . . . entrance
insalata, l' . . . . salad
inserire . . . . to insert
inverno, l' . . . . winter
io I
  io sono . . . . I am
Italia . . . . Italy
Italiani, gli . . . . Italians
italiano . . . . Italian

L

l' . . . . the
lampada, la . . . . lamp
latte, il . . . . milk
latteria, la . . . . dairy
lavanderia, la . . . . laundry
lavandino, il . . . . sink
lavare . . . . to wash
legume, il . . . . vegetable
leggere . . . . to read
lei . . . . she
Lei . . . . you
lentamente . . . . slowly
lento . . . . slow
lettera, la . . . . letter
letto, il . . . . bed
lezione, la . . . . lesson, lecture
libro, il . . . . book
lì . . . . there
libreria, la . . . . bookstore
linea, la (le linee) . . . . line
lira . . . . . . Italian unit of currency
lista, la . . . . list, menu
litro, il (i litri) . . . . liter
lo . . . . it, the
loro . . . . they
luce, la . . . . light
luglio . . . . July
lui . . . . he, him
lunedì . . . . Monday
lunga, lungo . . . . long
loro . . . . they

M

ma . . . . but
macchina, la . . . . car

macchina da noleggiare, la ... rental car
macchina fotografica, la .... camera
macelleria, la .... butcher shop
madre, la .... mother
maggio .... May
maggioranza, la .... majority
maglia, la .... sweater
maiale, il .... pork
malato .... sick
male .... bad
mancia, la .... tip
mandare .... to send
mangiare .... to eat
mano, la .... hand
manzo, il .... beef
marciapiede, il ...... railway platform
marrone .... brown
marzo .... March
martedì .... Tuesday
matita, la .... pencil
mattina, la .... morning
medico, il .... physician
meglio .... better
mela, la (le mele) .... apple
meno .... less, minus
meno un quarto .... a quarter to
menu, il .... menu
mercato, il .... market
mercoledì .... Wednesday
mese, il, (i mesi) .... month
metro, il (i metri) ...... meter
metro, la; metropolitana, la .... subway
mezzanotte, la .... midnight
mezzo .... middle
mezzogiorno, il .... noon
mi scusi .... excuse me
mila .... two or more thousand
milione .... million
mille .... one thousand
minestra, la (le ministre) .... soup
minuto, il, (i minuti) ...... minute
molto .... very
momento, il .... moment
  Un momento! .... Just a moment!
moneta, il (i monete) ...... coin
montagne, le .... mountain
mostrare .... to show
multicolore .... multi-colored
multa .... traffic fine
museo, il .... museum
mutande, le .... underpants

N

nave, la .... ship
neanche .... either
nebbia, la .... fog
necessario .... necessary
negozio, il (i negozi) ...... store
nel, nella .... in the
nero .... black
nevica .... it snows
niente .... nothing
nome, il (i nomi) .... name
noi .... we
non .... not, no
nonna, la .... grandmother
nonni, i .... grandparents
nonno, il .... grandfather
nord, il .... north
  del nord .... northern
notte, la .... night
novanta .... ninety
nove .... nine
novembre .... November
numero, il (i numeri) .... number
nuova, nuovo .... new

O

o .... or
occhiali, gli .... eyeglasses
occupato .... occupied
oggi .... today
ogni .... each, every
oltrepassa .... goes beyond
ombrello, l' .... umbrella
opera, l' .... opera
operatore, l' ...... telephone operator
ora, la (le ore) .... hour
orario, l' .... timetable
ordinare .... to order
orologeria, l' ....
.... clock and watchmaker's shop
l'orologio (gli orologi) ...... clock
ospedale, l' .... hospital
ostello della gioventù, l' ... youth hostel
osteria, l' .... cafe
ottanta .... eighty
otto .... eight
ottobre .... October
ovest, l' .... west
  dell'ovest .... western

P

padre, il .... father
pagare .... to pay
pagina, la .... page
paio, il .... pair
palazzo, il .... palace
palla, la .... ball
pane, il .... bread
panificio, il .... bakery
pantofole, le .... slippers
pantaloni, i .... trousers
paragrafo, il .... paragraph
parcheggio, il .... parking lot
parco, il .... park
parenti, i .... relatives
parete, la .... wall
parlare .... to speak
parola, la (le parole) ...... word
parole crociate ...... crossword puzzle
parrucchiere, il .... hairdresser
partenza, la .... departure
partire .... to leave
passaporto, il .... passport
pastasciutta, la .... pasta
pasticceria, la .... pastry shop
pasto, il .... meal
pellicola, la .... film
penna, la .... pen
pepe, il .... pepper
per .... for
per favore, per piacere ...... please
perchè .... why
perdere .... to lose
persona, la (le persone) ...... person
pesce, il .... fish
pescheria, la .... fish market
pettine, il .... comb
pezzo, il .... piece
piacere, il .... pleasure
  per piacere .... if you please
  Molto piacere ....
.... "It's a pleasure to meet you."
piano .... softly
piano, il .... floor
pianta, la .... map
pianterreno, il .... ground floor
piatto, il .... plate, dish
la piazza .... plaza, town square
piccole .... little
piede, il (i piedi) ...... foot
pigiama, il .... pajamas
pila, la .... battery

Q

quadro, il .... picture
qual .... what, which
quando .... when
quanto .... how much
quaranta .... forty
quarto, un .... quarter
  e un quarto .... a quarter past
  meno un quarto .... a quarter to
quattordici .... fourteen
quattro .... four
queste .... these
questo .... this
questura, la .... police station
qui .... here
quindici .... fifteen

piove .... it rains
pittura, la .... paint
più .... more
più tardi .... later
poco .... little
poi .... then
polizia, la .... police
pollame, il .... poultry
pomeriggio, il .... afternoon
porta, la .... door
portafoglio, il .... wallet
possibilità, la .... possibility
possono/potere ...... can/to be able to
posta, la .... mail, post office
posteggio, il ...... parking place
posto, il .... seat
potere .... to be able to/can
povero .... poor
PPTT, le .... post office
pranzo, il .... lunch
precedente .... preceding
prego .... you're welcome
premere .... to press
prenda .... take
prenotare .... to reserve/to book
prenotazioni, le .... reservations
prepararmi .... to prepare for me
preposizioni, le .... prepositions
prezzo, il .... price
prima classe, la .... first class
prima colazione, la ..... breakfast
primavera, la .... spring
priorità .... yield
profumo, il .... perfume
pronto .... prompt, ready
  "Pronto!" ....
.... "Hello!" (when answering telephone)
prosciutto, il .... ham
prossima .... next
protestante .... Protestant
puliti .... clean
pulsante, il .... push button
può/potere .... can/to be able to

R

ragazza, la .... girl
ragazzo, il .... boy
rapido .... rapid, fast
rapido, il ...... very fast train
rasoio, il .... razor
reggipetto, il .... brassière
religione, la (le religioni) ...... religion
restare .... to remain, to stay
reparto, il .... department
ricco .... rich
ricevitore, il ..... receiver (telephone)
ricevuta, la .... receipt
ripeta/ripetere ..... repeat/to repeat
riso, il .... rice
risponda/rispondere . respond/to respond
risposta, la (le risposte) ...... answer
ristorante, il .... restaurant

ritardo . . . . late
rivista, la . . . . magazine
Roma . . . . Rome
rosa, la (le rose) . . . . rose
rosa . . . . pink
rossi, rosso . . . . red

S

sabato . . . . Saturday
sala d'aspetto, la . . . . waiting room
sala da pranzo, la . . . . dining room
salata . . . . salted, salty
sale, il . . . . salt
Sali e Tabacchi, i . salt and tobacco store
salire . . . . to board/to climb into
salotto, il . . . . living room
salsiccia, la . . . . sausage
salumeria, la . . . . delicatessen
salumi, i . . . . sausages, salami
salute, la . . . . health
saluto, il (i saluti) . . . . greeting
sandalo, il (i sandali) . . . . sandal
sangue, il . . . . blood
sapere . . to know (a fact, an address, etc.)
sapone, il . . . . soap
sarta, la . . . . seamstress
sarto, il . . . . tailor
sbarcare . . . . to disembark
scala, la (le scale) . . . . . . staircase, stairs
la Scala . . . . Milanese opera house
scala mobile, la . . . . escalator
scarpa, la (le scarpe) . . . . shoe
scendere . . . . to get out/go down
scompartimento, lo . . . . . . compartment
scrivania, la . . . . desk
scrivere . . . . to write
scuola, la . . . . school
secco . . . . dry
seconda . . . . second
seconda classe, la . . . . second class
sedia, la . . . . chair
sedici . . . . sixteen
seduto . . . . seated
segnale, il . . . . signal, sign
segretario, il . . . . secretary
seguente, seguenti . . . . following
sei . . . . six
semplice . . simple, easy, one-way (ticket)
senso unico, il . . . . one-way street
sera, la . . . . evening
servizio, il . . . . service
sessanta . . . . sixty
settanta . . . . seventy
sette . . . . seven
settembre . . . . September
settimana, la (le settimane) . . . . . . week
sí . . . . yes
signora, la (le signore) . . . . lady
signore, il (i signori) . . . . . . gentleman
simile, simili . . . . similar
similitudine, la (le similitudini) . . . .
. . . . similarity
sinistra . . . . left
a sinistra . . . . to the left
sofà, il . . . . sofa
soffitto, il . . . . the ceiling
soggetto, il . . . . subject
solamente . . . . only
somma, la . . . . sum
sono . . . . they are
sopra . . . . over, above
soprabito, il . . . . coat
sorella, la . . . . sister
sorpresa, la . . . . surprise
sottile . . . . thin
sotto . . . . under, below
sottoveste, la . . . . slip
spazzolino da denti, lo . . . . . toothbrush
specchio, lo . . . . mirror

specialità, le . . . . specialities
spesso . . . . often
spiaggia, la . . . . beach
sportello, lo . . . . ticket window
squisito . . . . delicious
stagioni, le . . . . seasons
stanco . . . . tired
stanza, la . . . . room
stanza da bagno, la . . . . bathroom
Stati Uniti, gli . . . . United States
stazione di benzina, la . . . . . gas station
stazione dei treni, la . . . . . train station
stivale, lo (gli stivali) . . . . boot
strada, la . . . . street
straniero, lo . . . . stranger, foreigner
straordinario . . . . extraordinary
su . . . . on
Sua, Suo . . . . your
subito . . . . immediately
succede . . . . happening
Che succede? . . . . . . What's happening?
succo, il . . . . juice
succo di arancia, il . . . . . . orange juice
succo di pompelmo, il . grapefruit juice
sud, il . . . . south
del sud . . . . southern
sugo, il . . . . sauce
sul, sulla . . . . on the
supermercato, il . . . . grocery store
sveglia, la . . . . alarm clock

T

tabacco, il . . . . tobacco
taglia, la . . . . size
tagliano . . . . cut
tappeto, il . . . . carpet
tariffa, la . . . . fare
tassì, il . . . . taxi
tavolo, il . . . . table
tavola calda, la . . . . cafeteria
tazza, la (le tazze) . . . . cup
tè, il . . . . tea
teatro, il . . . . theater
telefono, il . . . . telephone
telefonata, la . . . . telephone call
telefonata interurbana, la . . . .
. . . . long-distance call
telegramma, il . . . . telegram
televisore, il . . . . television
temperatura, la (le temperature) . . . .
. . . . temperature
tempo, il . . . . weather, time
tendina, la . . . . curtain
termometro, il . . . . thermometer
tintoria, la . . . . dry cleaner's
tipiche . . . . typical
torre, la . . . . tower
La Torre Pendente . . . .
. . . . Leaning Tower of Pisa
tovagliolo, il . . . . napkin
tram, il . . . . tram, street car
trattoria, la . . . . restaurant
trasporto, il . . . . transportation
tre . . . . three
tredici . . . . thirteen
treno, il (i treni) . . . . train
trenta . . . . thirty
trovare . . . . to find
turista, il . . . . tourist
tutto . . . . everything

U

ufficio, l' . . . . office
ufficio oggetti smarriti . . . .
. . . . lost-and-found office
ufficio di cambio, l' . . . .
. . . . money-exchange office
ufficio deposito bagagli, l' . . . .
. . . . left-luggage office

ufficio informazioni . . . information office
ufficio postale italiano, l' . . . . . post office
un, un', una, uno . . . . a
undici . . . . eleven
unico . . . . unique, only, single
senso unico . . . . . . one-way (traffic sign)
università, l' . . . . university
uno . . . . one
uomo, l' (gli uomini) . . . . man
uova, le . . . . eggs
uova affogate, le . . . . poached egg
uova fritte, le . . . . fried egg
uova strapazzate, le . . . . scrambled egg
uscire . . . . to go out
uscita, l' . . . . exit
uscita principale, l' . . . . main exit
uscita di sicurezza, l' . . emergency exit
usuale . . . . usual, customary

V

vacanze, le . . . . vacation
fare le vacanze . . . . . to take a vacation
vada/andare . . . . go/to go
vagone letto, il . . . . sleeping car
vagone ristorante, il . . . . dining car
valigia, la . . . . suitcase
vaniglia, la . . . . vanilla
vaso, il . . . . vase
vecchia, vecchio . . . . old
vedere . . . . to see
veloce . . . . fast
vendere . . . . to sell
venditore, il . . . . vendor, seller
venerdì . . . . Friday
venire . . . . to come
venti . . . . twenty
vento, il . . . . windy
tira vento . . . . it's windy
verbo, il (i verbi) . . . . verb
verde . . . . green
verdure, le . . . . vegetables
vestiti, i . . . . clothing
vestito, il . . . . dress
via . . . . by
via, la . . . . way
via aerea . . . . air mail
viaggia . . . . travel, travels
viaggiatore, il . . . . traveler
viaggio, il . . . . trip
vicino . . . . near
viene/venire . . . . . come, comes/to come
vietato . . . . prohibited
vietato l'ingresso . . . . do not enter
vigoroso . . . . vigorous
vino, il . . . . wine
vino della casa, il . . . . house wine
violetto . . . . violet
visita, la . . . . visit
fare una vista . . . . to pay a visit
vitello, il . . . . veal
volare . . . . to fly/go by plane
volere . . . . would like
volo, il . . . . flight
vorrei/volere . . . . . I would like/would like
vorremmo/volere . . . .
. . . . we would like/would like

W

W.C., il . . . . water closet

Z

zaino, lo . . . . backpack
zero, lo . . . . zero
zia, la . . . . aunt
zio, lo . . . . uncle
zoo, lo . . . . zoo
zuppa, la (le zuppe) . . . . soup

DRINKING GUIDE

This guide is intended to explain the sometimes overwhelming variety of beverages available to you while in Italy. It is by no means complete. Some of the experimenting has been left up to you, but this should get you started. The asterisks (*) indicate brand names.

BEVANDE CALDE (hot drinks)

caffè (espresso)	espresso coffee
caffelatte	coffee with milk
cappuccino	coffee topped with steamed milk
caffè macchiato	coffee with a little milk or cream
caffè americano	American coffee
tè	tea
con limone	with lemon
con latte	with milk
cioccolata	hot chocolate

BEVANDE FREDDE (cold drinks)

latte freddo	cold milk
frappé	milk shake
acqua minerale	mineral water
*San Pellegrino	
*Recoaro	
*Montecatini	
aranciata	orangeade
limonata	lemon drink
spremuta di limone	lemonade
succo di frutta	fruit juice
amarena	cherry syrup drink
orzata	almond syrup drink
gassosa	carbonated soft drink
tè freddo	iced tea
caffè freddo	iced coffee

APERITIVI (aperitifs) These may be enjoyed straight or over ice.

sherry	sherry
porto	port
*Martini bianco	white vermouth
*Martini rosso	red vermouth
*Pernod	anise base
*Campari	
*Cinzano	
*Punt e Mes	

BIRRE (beers) There is not a great variety of beers in Italy. **La birra** is purchased in **bottiglia** (bottle).

*Peroni
*Italia

VINI (wines) There is a very wide variety of wines in Italy and you will want to try many of them. Each region produces its own wine, ranging in taste from very sweet to very dry. You may drink wine by the **bicchiere** (glass), **litro** (liter), **mezzo litro** (half liter) or the **bottiglia** (bottle).

vino rosso	red wine
vino bianco	white wine
vino rosè	rosè wine
spumante	sparkling wine
vino ordinario	table wine
vino da tavola	table wine
vino della casa	house wine
vino locale	local wine of the region
dolce	sweet
amabile	between sweet and dry
secco	dry

WINE	REGION	COLOR	TASTE
*Barbera	Emilia	rosso	secco/amabile
*Barolo	Piemonte	rosso	secco
*Chianti	Toscana	rosso	secco
*Lambrusco	Emilia	rosso	secco/amabile
*Verdicchio	le Marche	bianco	secco
marsala siciliano	Sicilia	rosso	dolce
moscato	Toscana	bianco	dolce

ALCOOL (spirits) Cocktail drinking is not widespread in Italy. The following are available in large, international hotels and **"bar americani."**

gin	gin
bourbon	bourbon
rum	rum
vodka	vodka
whisky	scotch
martini dry	American martini

DIGESTIVI (liqueurs, brandies)

acquavite	natural grain spirits
grappa	wine brandy
*Fernet-Branca	herb base
*Alpestre	herb base
*Ferro China	bark base
*Amaretto	almond base
*Sambuca	anise base
con la mosca	with a coffee bean
*Drambuie	
*Cointreau	
*Grand Marnier	

112 **IL GHIACCIO** . . . . ice

Il Menu

Preparazione (preparation)

cotto	cooked
crudo	raw
arrosto	roast
fritto	fried
al forno	baked
alla griglia, ai ferri	grilled
allo spiedo	roasted on a spit
bollito	boiled
affumicato	smoked
alla brace	charcoal-broiled
farcito	stuffed
al sangue	rare
al punto	medium
ben cotto	well-done

Altri (others)

marmellata	jam
miele	honey
sale	salt
pepe	pepper
olio	oil
aceto	vinegar
senape/mostarda	mustard
riso	rice
pane	bread
formaggio	cheese
dolci	pastry and dessert
torta	cake
dolce	pastry
gelato	ice cream
panna montata	whipped cream

FOLD HERE

Insalata (salad)

verde	tossed green salad
capricciosa	mixed vegetables, with ham in mayonnaise sauce
di pesce	boiled fish
di riso	cold rice, vegetables, seafood, mayonnaise
russa	vegetables, hard-boiled eggs, mayonnaise
viennese	tuna, hard-boiled eggs, beans, olives

Riso, Risotto (rice)

alla milanese	with saffron
con funghi	with mushrooms
alla marinara	tomato sauce, clams, prawns
Risi e Bisi	rice and peas
Suppli	deep-fried rice balls

Frutta (fruit)

mela	apple
pera	pear
albicocca	apricot
pesca	peach
banana	banana
arancia	orange
mandarino	tangerine
ciliege	cherries
cocomero	watermelon
prugna	plum
uva	grapes
uva passa	raisins
dattero	date
noce di cocco	coconut
limone	lemon
ananas	pineapple
pompelmo	grapefruit
fichi	figs
fragole	strawberries
lamponi	raspberries
mirtilli	blueberries
macedonia di frutta	fruit salad
misto bosco	mixed berries

Buon appetito!

FOLD HERE

Pesci e Frutti di Mare (fish and seafood)

acciughe	anchovies
anguilla	eel
aragosta	lobster
calamari	squid
cefalo	gray mullet
gamberi	shrimp or prawns
granchio	crab
merluzzo	codfish
muscoli	mussels
persico	perch
pesce spada	swordfish
polipo	octopus
rane	frogs
salmone	salmon
sardine	sardines
sogliola	sole
spigola	sea bass
storione	sturgeon
tonno	tuna
triglie	red mullet
trota	trout
vongole	clams

Verdure (vegetables)

cipolle	onions
piselli	green peas
pomodori	tomatoes
fagiolini	string beans
cavolfiore	cauliflower
carciofo	artichokes
carote	carrots
asparagi	asparagus
spinaci	spinach
lenticchie	lentils
funghi	mushrooms
broccoli	broccoli
finocchio	fennel
melanzane	eggplant
olive	olives
patate	potatoes
peperoni	bell peppers
porri	leeks
prezzemolo	parsley
rapanelli	radishes
sedano	celery
zucca	yellow squash
zucchini	zucchini
misto di verdure	mixed cooked vegetables

Antipasti (appetizers)

acciughe	anchovies
di mare	seafood with lemon-juice dressing
misto	mixed appetizers
bagna cauda	raw vegetables dipped in dressing
frutti di mare	seafood
gamberi	shrimps and prawns
lumache	snails
ostriche	oysters
peperonata	sliced peppers, onions and tomatoes
mortadella	bologna
polipo	octopus
porchetta romana	stuffed pig
prosciutto	ham
salame	variety of sausages
salsicce	cooked sausage
tartufi	truffles

Minestre e Zuppe (soups)

minestrone	thick vegetable soup
minestrina	thin clear broth
zuppa di pesce	fish soup
brodo	broth
stracciatella	broth with beaten eggs and Parmesan
pavese	broth with poached egg on fried bread

Pastasciutta (pasta)

spaghetti	long, solid-core pasta
fettucine	flat noodle
ravioli	stuffed pasta, small and usually square
lasagne	baked, layered casserole
cannelloni	stuffed cylinder-shaped pasta
tortellini	small stuffed pasta, often in soups
vermicelli	very thin pasta
cannolo	short tubes of macaroni
cappelletti	round, cap-shaped pasta
conchiglie	shell-shaped pasta
farfallette	butterfly-shaped pasta
fusilli	spiral-shaped pasta
gnocchi	small dumpling
linguine	narrow, flat noodles
penne	hollow pasta, cut diagonally
rigatoni	large, hollow pasta

Sugo di Carne (meat sauces)

alla bolognese	meat sauce used most often in America
alla romagnola	tomato sauce with garlic and parsley
alla carbonara	sauce of eggs, bacon and garlic
alla fiorentina	herbal meat sauce with green peas
all'arrabbiata	herbal tomato sauce of bacon, sausage and cayenne
alla piemontese	herbal meat sauce with nutmeg and truffles
alla romana	seasoned meat sauce

Senza Carne (meatless sauces)

aglio e olio	olive oil and garlic
alla besciamella	creamed white sauce
al burro	butter and Parmesan
alla Campagnola	mushrooms, tomatoes and herbs
alla Crema	white sauce with egg yolk and Parmesan
alla Genovese	basil, garlic and pine nuts
alla Napolitana	tomatoes, basil and Parmesan
al Pomodoro	herbal tomato sauce

Frutti di Mare (seafood sauces)

alla Boscaiola	tuna, anchovies, tomatoes, and mushrooms
ai Frutti di Mare	herbs, tomatoes and seafoods
al Tonno	tuna, garlic, tomatoes and capers
di Magro	tuna, anchovies and herbs
alla Posillipo	herbs, tomatoes and seafood
alle Vongole	clams and garlic, with or without tomatoes

Carne (meat)

Cacciagione (wild game)

anitra	duck
cervo	deer
coniglio	rabbit
lepre	hare
tordo	thrush

Pollame (poultry)

pollo, gallina	chicken
tacchino	turkey
faraona	guinea fowl
cappone	capon
piccione	pigeon
quaglie	quail
fagiano	pheasant

Vitello (veal)

bianchette di vitello	veal stew with gravy
bistecca di vitello	loin veal steak
costoletta di vitello	veal chop or steak
cotoletta	veal steak without bone
alla Milanese	breaded veal cutlets
lombata di vitello	loin of veal
lingua di vitello	tongue
noce di vitello	sirloin of veal
rollatine di vitello	rolled veal steak
spalla di vitello al forno	roast shoulder of veal
rollata al forno	rolled stuffed breast of veal
rognone di vitello	kidney

Agnello (lamb)

abbacchio	milk-fed lamb
braciolette d'abbacchio	grilled lamb chops or cutlets
abbacchio al forno	roasted lamb
costole alla Milanese	fried breaded lamb chops
tracciole d'agnello	like shish kebab

Manzo (beef)

bistecca alla Fiorentina	unboned rib steak
braciole	rib steak
entrecote	boneless rib steak
fegato	liver
cervella	brains
lingua di bue	beef tongue
stracotto	stew
trippe	tripe

Maiale (pork)

arista di maiale	roast loin of pork
arrostino alla salvia	roast pork with sage
arrosto di porchetta	stuffed roast suckling pig
zampe di maiale	pig's feet

(veh-nee-reh) **venire**	*(kee-ah-mahr-see)* **chiamarsi**
(ahn-dah-reh) **andare**	*(kohm-prah-reh)* **comprare**
(ah-veh-reh) **avere**	*(pahr-lah-reh)* **parlare**
(eem-pah-rah-reh) **imparare**	*(ah-bee-tah-reh)* **abitare**
(voh-reh-ee) **vorrei**	*(ohr-dee-nah-reh)* **ordinare**
(ah-veh-reh) *(bee-sohn-yoh)* *(dee)* **avere bisogno di**	*(reh-stah-reh)* **restare**

to be called	to come
to buy	to go
to speak	to have
to live/reside	to learn
to order	I would like
to stay/remain	to need

(dee-reh) **dire**	*(vehn-deh-reh)* **vendere**
(mahn-jah-reh) **mangiare**	*(veh-deh-reh)* **vedere**
(beh-reh) **bere**	*(mahn-dah-reh)* **mandare**
(ah-spet-tah-reh) **aspettare**	*(dohr-mee-reh)* **dormire**
(kah-pee-reh) **capire**	*(troh-vah-reh)* **trovare**
(ree-peh-teh-reh) **ripetere**	*(fah-reh)* **fare**

to sell	to say
to see	to eat
to send	to drink
to sleep	to wait
to find	to understand
to do/make	to repeat

(skree-veh-reh)
scrivere

(leh-jeh-reh)
leggere

(moh-strah-reh)
mostrare

(vee-ah-jah-reh)
viaggiare

(pah-gah-reh)
pagare

(lah-voh-rah-reh)
lavorare

(poh-teh-reh)
potere

(ahn-dah-reh) *(een)* *(ah-air-ree-oh)*
andare in aereo

(doh-veh-reh)
dovere

(chee) *(voo-oh-leh)* *(vohl-yoh-noh)*
ci vuole/ci vogliono

(sah-peh-reh)
sapere

(fah-reh) *(lah)* *(vah-lee-jah)*
fare la valigia

to read	to write
to travel	to show
to work	to pay
to fly/go by plane	to be able to/can
it takes	to have to/must/owe
to pack	to know

(pahr-tee-reh) **partire**	*(kee-oo-deh-reh)* **chiudere**
(gwee-dah-reh) **guidare**	*(lah-vah-reh)* **lavare**
(foo-mah-reh) **fumare**	*(kahm-bee-ah-reh)* **cambiare**
(doh-mahn-dah-reh) **domandare**	*(pehr-deh-reh)* **perdere**
(neh-vee-kah) **nevica**	*(ee-oh)* *(soh-noh)* **(io) sono**
(pee-oh-veh) **piove**	*(noh-ee)* *(see-ah-moh)* **(noi) siamo**

to close	to depart/leave
to wash	to drive
to exchange/change	to smoke
to lose	to ask
I am	it is snowing
we are	it is raining

(een-koh-meen-chah-reh) **incominciare**	*(prehn-deh-reh)* **prendere**
(ah-pree-reh) **aprire**	*(sah-lee-reh)* **salire**
(koo-chee-nah-reh) **cucinare**	*(shen-deh-reh)* **scendere**
(aht-tehr-rah-reh) **atterrare**	*(en-trah-reh)* **entrare**
(preh-noh-tah-reh) **prenotare**	*(kahm-bee-ah-reh)* **cambiare**
(koh-stah-reh) **costare**	*(ahr-ree-vah-reh)* **arrivare**

to take	to begin
to climb/board	to open
to go down/get out	to cook
to enter	to land
to transfer	to book/reserve
to arrive	to cost

(bwoh-noh)   *(kaht-tee-voh)*
buono - cattivo

(veh-loh-cheh)   *(rah-pee-doh)*   *(len-toh)*
veloce/rapido - lento

(pee-ah-noh)   *(fohr-teh)*
piano - forte

(grohs-soh)   *(soht-tee-leh)*
grosso - sottile

(grahn-deh)   *(peek-koh-loh)*
grande - piccolo

(mohl-toh)   *(poh-koh)*
molto - poco

(kahl-doh)   *(frehd-doh)*
caldo - freddo

(ah-pehr-toh)   *(kee-oo-soh)*
aperto - chiuso

(see-nee-strah)   *(deh-strah)*
sinistra - destra

(dohl-cheh)   *(ah-groh)*
dolce - agro

(soh-prah)   *(soht-toh)*
sopra - sotto

(mee)   *(skoo-see)*   *(pehr-mess-soh)*
mi scusi - permesso

fast - slow	good - bad
thick - thin	soft - loud
much - little	large - small
open - closed	warm - cold
sweet - sour	left - right
excuse me	above - below

(loo-ee) **lui** *(leh-ee)* **lei** } **è**	*(ahl-toh)* *(bahs-soh)* **alto - basso**
(leh-ee) *(eh)* **Lei è**	*(poh-veh-roh)* *(reek-koh)* **povero - ricco**
(loh-roh) *(soh-noh)* **loro sono**	*(kohr-toh)* *(loon-goh)* **corto - lungo**
(ahr-ree-veh-dehr-chee) **arrivederci**	*(mah-lah-toh)* **malato -** *(dee)* *(bwoh-nah)* *(sah-loo-teh)* **di buona salute**
(cheh) *(chee)* *(soh-noh)* **c'è / ci sono**	*(eh-koh-noh-mee-koh)* *(kah-roh)* **economico - caro**
(koh-meh) *(vah)* **Come va?**	*(vek-kee-oh)* *(joh-vah-neh)* **vecchio - giovane**

high - low	he $\rbrace$ is she
poor - rich	you are
short - long	they are
sick - healthy	good-bye
cheap - expensive	there is/there are
old - young	How are you?

Now that you've finished...

Congratulations

You've done it!

You've completed all 23 Steps, stuck your labels, flashed your cards and clipped your menu. Do you realize how far you've come and how much you've learned? In a short period of time, you have accomplished what it sometimes takes years to achieve in a traditional language class.

You can now confidently

- ask questions,
- understand directions,
- make reservations,
- order food and
- shop anywhere.

And you can do it all in a foreign language! This means you can now go anywhere - from a large cosmopolitan restaurant to a small, out-of-the-way village where no one speaks English. Your experiences will be much more enjoyable and worry-free now that you speak the language, understand what is being said and know something of the culture.

Yes, learning a foreign language can be fun. And no, not everyone abroad speaks English.

Kristine Kershul

Kristine Kershul

Have a wonderful time, whether your trip is to Europe, the Orient or simply across the border.

REORDER FORM

Please send me the following titles from the series.

Title	Quantity	Price Each	Total
CHINESE		US $12.95	
FRENCH		US $12.95	
GERMAN		US $12.95	
INGLES		US $12.95	
ITALIAN		US $12.95	
JAPANESE		US $12.95	
NORWEGIAN		US $12.95	
RUSSIAN		US $12.95	
SPANISH		US $12.95	
	Shipping*		2.00
PREFERRED READER	WA residents add tax		
	Total Order		

PLEASE CHECK: *On foreign orders add $7.50 for airmail shipment.*

☐ Bill my credit card account ☐ VISA ☐ MC ☐ AMEX

no._____ exp. date_____ / _____

☐ My check for $_____ is enclosed.

Name _____

Address _____

City_____ State_____ Zip_____

Telephone No. (_____) _____

REORDER FORM

Please send me the following titles from the series.

Title	Quantity	Price Each	Total
CHINESE		US $12.95	
FRENCH		US $12.95	
GERMAN		US $12.95	
INGLES		US $12.95	
ITALIAN		US $12.95	
JAPANESE		US $12.95	
NORWEGIAN		US $12.95	
RUSSIAN		US $12.95	
SPANISH		US $12.95	
	Shipping*		2.00
PREFERRED READER	WA residents add tax		
	Total Order		

PLEASE CHECK: *On foreign orders add $7.50 for airmail shipment.*

☐ Bill my credit card account ☐ VISA ☐ MC ☐ AMEX

no._____ exp. date_____ / _____

☐ My check for $_____ is enclosed.

Name _____

Address _____

City_____ State_____ Zip_____

Telephone No. (_____) _____

Coming soon...

Published
Feb. 1984